VIRGINIA
COOK BOOK

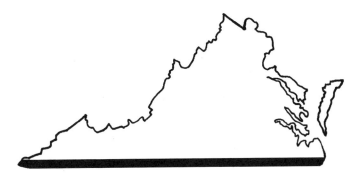

Compiled by
Janice Therese Mancuso

Cooking Across America Cookbook Collection™

GOLDEN WEST ✦ PUBLISHERS

About
Janice Therese Mancuso

Janice Therese Mancuso is also the author of *Herbed-Wine Cuisine, Creating and Cooking with Herb Infused Wines.* She owns a specialty food company, develops recipes for food manufacturers and is a cooking instructor. She publishes *Simply Elegant,* a quarterly newsletter on food, decorating and entertaining; writes a monthly on-line column for the MyCookbook website and writes for various food publications.

Visit Janice's website: www.jtmancuso.com.

ISBN – 1-885590-45-8

Printed in the United States of America

5th Printing © 2004

Golden West Publishers, Inc.
4113 N. Longview Ave.
Phoenix, AZ 85014, USA
(800) 658-5830

For free sample recipes and complete Table of Contents for every Golden West cookbook, visit our website: **goldenwestpublishers.com**

Table of Contents

Table of Contents *(Continued)*

Welcome to Virginia!

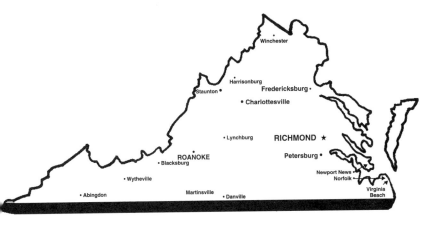

Introduction

As the birthplace of eight United States presidents, no other state offers Virginia's historical legacy. From majestic mountain ranges to coastal backdrops, Virginia is home to rich history and great food. As one of the largest seafood suppliers in the nation, Virginia's nutrient rich Chesapeake Bay rewards us with premier crabs, oysters and a variety of fish. In addition to seafood, Virginia Cook Book features savory ham dishes, delicious Shenandoah Valley apple recipes, tempting peanut delights and a cornucopia of historical and family favorites.

Virginia Cook Book is brimming with tasty recipes contributed by residents of "The Old Dominion." From Abingdon to Waynesboro, these recipes reflect the many flavors of Virginia and highlight its celebrated heritage.

Enjoy these tastes of Virginia!

Virginia Facts

Size – 10th largest state with an area of 40,817 square miles
Population – 6,791,345 (1998)
State Capital – Richmond
Statehood – June 25, 1788, the 10th state
    admitted to the Union
State Nickname – The Old Dominion;
    Mother of Presidents
State Song – "Carry Me Back to Old
    Virginia" by James A. Bland
State Motto – *Sic Semper Tyrannis*
    (Thus always to tyrants).
State Dog – American Foxhound
State Shell – Oyster Shell
State Bird – Cardinal

State Tree
Flowering Dogwood

State Flower
Flowering Dogwood

Famous Virginians

Richard Arlen, actor; **Arthur Ashe,** tennis player; **Pearl Bailey,** singer; **Russell Baker,** columnist; **Warren Beatty,** actor; **George Bingham,** painter; **Richard E. Byrd,** polar explorer; **Willa Cather,** novelist; **Roy Clark,** country music artist; **William Clark,** explorer; **Henry Clay,** statesman; **Joseph Cotten,** actor; **Ella Fitzgerald,** singer; **William H. Harrison,** former president; **Patrick Henry,** statesman; **Sam Houston,** political leader; **Thomas Jefferson,** former president; **Robert E. Lee,** Confederate general; **Meriwether Lewis,** explorer; **Shirley MacLaine,** actress; **James Madison,** former president; **John Marshall,** jurist; **Cyrus McCormick,** inventor; **James Monroe,** former president; **Opechancanough,** Powhatan leader; **John Payne,** actor; **Walter Reed,** army surgeon; **Matthew Ridgway,** former Army Chief of Staff; **Bill "Bojangles" Robinson,** dancer; **George C. Scott,** actor; **Sam Snead,** golfer; **James "Jeb" Stuart,** Confederate army officer; **Zachary Taylor,** former president; **Nat Turner,** leader of slave uprising; **John Tyler,** former president; **Booker T. Washington,** educator; **George Washington,** first president; **Woodrow Wilson,** former president.

Virginia Visitor Information: (804) 786-4484 or (800) 932-5827

Appetizers

Crispy Clam Pinwheels

20 thin slices fresh WHITE BREAD
1 med. ONION, finely chopped
3 Tbsp. BUTTER or MARGARINE
1/4 cup FLOUR
2 cans (6.5 oz. ea.) CLAMS, undrained
2 cloves GARLIC, crushed
2 tsp. LEMON JUICE
2 tsp. minced fresh PARSLEY
1/2 tsp. freshly ground BLACK PEPPER
Melted BUTTER

Trim crusts from bread and flatten with a rolling pin. In a medium saucepan, sauté onion in butter until tender; stir in flour to thicken. Add clams and broth, garlic, lemon juice, parsley and pepper. Cook until mixture thickens, stirring occasionally (may have to add a little more flour). Spoon a strip of clam filling 1/3 up from the end of each slice of flattened bread. Bring short end of bread over filling and roll. Cut each roll into 4 pieces. Place each piece, cut side down, on a greased baking sheet and brush with melted butter. Bake at 375° about 12 minutes or until lightly browned.

Makes about 80 pinwheels.

Easy Blue Ridge Cheese Ball

William Barnhardt—Willaby's Fine Sauces, White Stone

2 pkgs. (8 oz. ea.) CREAM CHEESE, softened
1 jar (3 oz.) WILLABY'S® BLUE RIDGE BLUES SAUCE
4 Tbsp. chopped ONION
1/4 cup dried PARSLEY or chopped WALNUTS

Add first three ingredients to a mixing bowl and blend with an electric mixer. Scrape down sides to form somewhat of a ball in the bottom of the bowl. Refrigerate overnight. Remove mixture from bowl, form into a ball and sprinkle with parsley or nuts, patting lightly to cover. Place on a serving platter and surround with crackers.

Serves 25.

Did You Know?

Eight U. S. Presidents were born in Virginia!
William H. Harrison, Thomas Jefferson, James Madison, James Monroe, Zachary Taylor, John Tyler, George Washington and *Woodrow Wilson.*

Herbed Cheese Spread

Shenandoah Growers, Inc.—Harrisonburg

1 Tbsp. ea. chopped SHENANDOAH GROWERS® fresh
**   OREGANO, BASIL and DILL**
1 tsp. THYME
1 clove GARLIC, crushed
2 pkgs. (8 oz. ea.) CREAM CHEESE, softened
1 cup MARGARINE, softened
1/4 tsp. PEPPER

In a large bowl, blend all ingredients together. Refrigerate for 1/2 hour for flavors to blend. Serve as a dip for crackers or raw vegetables or spread on toasted bagels.

Serves 25.

Rowena's Crab Dip

"Red Lightning Hot Sauce will heat up everything, and everybody."

Rowena's, Inc.—Norfolk

1 pkg. (8 oz.) CREAM CHEESE, softened
5 to 6 Tbsp. ROWENA'S® RED LIGHTNING HOT SAUCE
1/2 lb. CRABMEAT
1/2 to 1 cup MAYONNAISE
VERMOUTH

In a medium bowl, blend cream cheese with sauce. Add crabmeat. Stir in enough mayonnaise and vermouth to thin. Use as a dip for crackers and raw vegetables.

Serves 10.

Chesapeake Bay Virginia Crab Puffs

"This is a family favorite."

Susan Longyear—Fairlea Farm Bed & Breakfast, Washington

1 lb. fresh or 1 can (14.5 oz.) CRABMEAT
1 cup MAYONNAISE
1/2 cup grated ONION
1 cup shredded CHEDDAR CHEESE
1 Tbsp. LEMON JUICE
Pinch of SALT
1 pkg. HOT DOG BUNS

In a large bowl, combine all ingredients except hot dog buns. Cut rounds from the buns using a small cookie cutter or the rim of a juice glass, cutting 3 from each half of the buns. Spread crab mixture evenly on top of rounds. Broil or bake at 400° for 5-10 minutes.

Makes 48 puffs.

Note: Puffs may be baked and frozen for later use. Before serving, reheat at 400° for about 10 minutes.

Hot Spinach & Artichoke Dip

"Each year our inn has guests attending the University of Virginia graduation exercises. In honor of the graduates, we serve something special during the afternoon refreshment time. This recipe was used for our own son's graduation party and has become a standard here at the inn."

Rebecca Lindway—The Inn at Monticello, Charlottesville

1 can (14 oz.) ARTICHOKE HEARTS
1 pkg. (10 oz.) frozen CHOPPED SPINACH
1 cup MAYONNAISE
1 cup SOUR CREAM
1/2 cup grated PARMESAN CHEESE
8 to 10 drops TABASCO®

Drain and chop artichoke hearts. Thaw and squeeze dry spinach. In a large bowl, blend mayonnaise, sour cream, Parmesan and Tabasco together. Fold in spinach and then artichoke hearts. Place mixture in an oiled casserole dish and bake at 350° for 30 minutes. Serve with crackers.

Serves 8.

Bacon & Tomato Cups

S. Wallace Edwards & Sons, Inc.—Surry

8 slices BACON, cooked and crumbled
1 med. TOMATO, coarsely chopped
1/2 sm. ONION, chopped
3/4 cup grated SWISS CHEESE
1/2 cup MAYONNAISE
1 tsp. BASIL
1 can (10 oz.) FLAKY BISCUITS

Preheat oven to 375°. Mix all ingredients together, except biscuits. Set aside. Separate each biscuit into 3 thin layers. Press each layer into mini-muffin pan cups and fill with bacon mixture. Bake for 10-12 minutes or until golden brown.

Makes 30 cups.

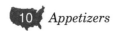

Edwards' Virginia Bacon & Mushroom Dip

S. Wallace Edwards & Sons, Inc.—Surry

10 slices EDWARDS'® VIRGINIA HICKORY-SMOKED BACON
8 oz. fresh MUSHROOMS, chopped
1/2 cup finely diced ONION
1 clove GARLIC, minced
2 Tbsp. FLOUR
1/2 tsp. SALT
1/8 tsp. ground BLACK PEPPER
1 pkg. (8 oz.) CREAM CHEESE, cubed
2 tsp. WORCESTERSHIRE SAUCE
1 tsp. SOY SAUCE
1/2 cup SOUR CREAM
1 to 2 tsp. minced fresh PARSLEY or CHIVES

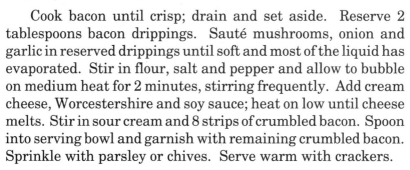

Cook bacon until crisp; drain and set aside. Reserve 2 tablespoons bacon drippings. Sauté mushrooms, onion and garlic in reserved drippings until soft and most of the liquid has evaporated. Stir in flour, salt and pepper and allow to bubble on medium heat for 2 minutes, stirring frequently. Add cream cheese, Worcestershire and soy sauce; heat on low until cheese melts. Stir in sour cream and 8 strips of crumbled bacon. Spoon into serving bowl and garnish with remaining crumbled bacon. Sprinkle with parsley or chives. Serve warm with crackers.

Makes 2 1/2 cups.

Historic Virginia

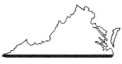

Virginia was named for Queen Elizabeth I of England (the Virgin Queen). King Charles II named it "Old Dominion" because it remained loyal to the crown during the English Civil War. In 1607, the first permanent English settlement in America was developed at Jamestown. All or part of eight other states were formed from western territory once claimed by Virginia. They are Illinois, Indiana, Kentucky, Michigan, Minnesota, Ohio, West Virginia and Wisconsin.

Edwards' Virginia Ham & Cheese Puffs

S. Wallace Edwards & Sons, Inc.—Surry

1/2 cup FLOUR
1/2 cup ground EDWARDS'® VIRGINIA HAM
1 1/4 cups grated SHARP CHEDDAR CHEESE
2 Tbsp. BUTTER, softened
1 to 2 Tbsp. WATER

Place all ingredients in a large bowl and mix with fingertips to make a stiff dough, adding water as necessary. Roll dough into balls approximately 3/4-inch in diameter. Place on a lightly greased cookie sheet and bake in a preheated oven at 400° for 12-14 minutes or until lightly browned. Serve hot.

Makes 20 to 24 puffs.

John Rolfe

One of the early colonists, John Rolfe, began growing tobacco. The export of that crop became an important source of income for all of the struggling colonists. In 1614, Rolfe's marriage to Pocahontas, daughter of an Indian chief, heralded a period of peace and prosperity.

Spicy Mango Salsa

Serve as a dip for boiled shrimp or grilled chicken pieces.

Developed for Millcroft Farms Co. by Janice Therese Mancuso

2 MANGOES peeled and chopped
1 med. TOMATO, chopped
1/3 cup chopped GREEN ONIONS
1/3 cup chopped JALAPEÑO PEPPER
3 Tbsp. MILLCROFT FARMS COMPANY® CORN COB JELLY
1/3 cup chopped CILANTRO

In a medium bowl, mix mangoes, tomato, green onions and peppers. Stir in jelly and cilantro. Let flavors blend about 1 hour before serving.

Makes about 3 cups.

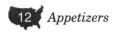

Jalapeño Jelly

"I love hot and spicy foods. This jelly is an old standby. It's great served with crackers and whipped cream cheese with just a hint of chili powder."

Rebecca Lindway—The Inn at Monticello, Charlottesville

3 lg. very ripe RED BELL PEPPERS, cored and seeded
6 to 8 JALAPEÑO CHILES, seeded
1 1/2 cups CIDER VINEGAR
6 1/2 cups SUGAR
2 pouches CERTO® FRUIT PECTIN

Using a food processor, finely chop bell peppers and jalapeños, then place in a large saucepan. Stir in vinegar and sugar. Boil, uncovered, for 30 minutes or until mixture is slightly thickened and peppers are clear. Remove from heat. Open pouches of pectin and quickly stir into peppers. Return to heat; bring to a full rolling boil and boil one minute. Remove from heat and skim off foam. Pour into sterile pint jars, add lids. Turn upside down for 1 hour, then turn right side up and store.

Makes 4 pints.

Chutney Cheese Spread

"This recipe came from a recipe exchange with friends. What a great recipe for blue cheese lovers!"

Bettie P. Shelton—Petersburg

1 pkg. (8 oz.) CREAM CHEESE, softened
1 pkg. (4 oz.) BLUE CHEESE, crumbled
1 cup APPLE PEPPER CHUTNEY

In a medium mixing bowl, combine the cheeses and 1/2 of the chutney; mix well. On a serving plate, form mixture into a ring. Spoon remaining chutney into the center of the ring. Serve with crackers.

Salmon Spread

"This is delicious as an appetizer or served on a
bed of lettuce as a tasty salad."

Meryl Bernstein—Richmond

1 can (14.75 oz.) SALMON, drained and boned
1 pkg. (8 oz.) CREAM CHEESE, softened
1 1/2 Tbsp. LEMON JUICE
2 tsp. grated ONION
1 tsp. WHITE HORSERADISH
1/2 tsp. SALT
1 1/4 tsp. LIQUID SMOKE

In a medium mixing bowl, combine all ingredients and mix
well. Chill overnight. Spread on cocktail ryes or crackers.

Crab Spread

1 can (6 oz.) CRABMEAT, drained and flaked
8 oz. SEAFOOD SAUCE
1 pkg. (8 oz.) CREAM CHEESE, softened

Blend crabmeat with seafood sauce. Place block of cream
cheese on a serving platter and top with crabmeat mixture.
Serve with crackers.

Oysters Parmesan

1 lg. ONION, minced
5 cloves GARLIC, minced
1/2 cup OLIVE OIL
1 pt. OYSTERS and liquor
1 1/4 cups SEASONED BREAD CRUMBS
1/4 cup grated PARMESAN CHEESE
4 strips BACON, cooked until crisp, crumbled

In a skillet, sauté onion and garlic in olive oil until slightly
brown; add oysters and cook until the edges curl. Remove from
heat; stir in bread crumbs, cheese, oyster liquor and bacon. Mix
well. Add mixture to individual ramekins and bake for 30
minutes at 350°.

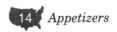

Lancaster County's Virginia Crab Dip

Dr. Frances N. Ashburn—Lancaster County School System,
Lancaster

1/2 stick BUTTER or MARGARINE
2/3 cup FLOUR
3 cups MILK
1 1/2 cups grated CHEESE
SALT and PEPPER to taste
1 lb. fresh CHESAPEAKE BAY BLUE CRABMEAT
1/4 cup SHERRY

In a double boiler, combine butter, flour, milk, cheese, salt and pepper. Cook on medium heat, stirring constantly, until mixture thickens. Add crabmeat and sherry; stir until blended. Pour into a heated chafing dish and serve with French bread chunks or crackers.

Did You Know?

Virginia, Kentucky, Massachusetts and Pennsylvania are the only states in the U.S. that are officially called "commonwealths."

Spinach Dip

"I made this dip for a 'Taste of Home' contest at my college and won!"

Meryl Bernstein—Richmond

2 pkgs. (10 oz. ea.) frozen SPINACH, thawed and drained
1 cup MAYONNAISE
1 cup SOUR CREAM
1 pkg. (1 oz.) HIDDEN VALLEY® RANCH DRESSING MIX

In a medium mixing bowl, combine all ingredients and mix well. Refrigerate overnight. Before serving, stir again. Serve with sliced raw vegetables.

Hot Virginia Dip

"This recipe has been served at Virginia High School League's State Basketball Tournaments for as long as I can remember. This dip originated with Anna Sanders, a teacher, principal, counselor and 'mom' to Lancaster High students for fifty years!"

Dr. Frances N. Ashburn—Lancaster County School System, Lancaster

1 cup chopped PECANS
2 tsp. BUTTER
2 pkgs. (8 oz. ea.) CREAM CHEESE, softened
4 Tbsp. MILK
1 cup SOUR CREAM
5 oz. DRIED BEEF, minced
1 tsp. GARLIC SALT
4 tsp. minced ONION

In a skillet, sauté pecans in butter; reserve. Mix remaining ingredients together. Pour into 1 1/2-quart baking dish. Top with pecans. Chill. When ready to serve, bake at 350° for 20 minutes. Serve hot with assorted crackers, chips or raw vegetables.

Shrimp Butter

"This is a family favorite I make for parties and get-togethers."

Linda W. Ayers—Goodview

1 pkg. (8 oz.) CREAM CHEESE, softened
1 stick BUTTER, softened
2-3 Tbsp. LEMON JUICE
4 Tbsp. MAYONNAISE
1 med. ONION, finely diced
1 can (4.25 oz.) TINY SHRIMP

In a food processor or blender, combine the cream cheese, butter, lemon juice and mayonnaise; blend until smooth. Add the onion and shrimp; stir until mixed. To serve, spread on crackers.

Breakfasts & Brunches

Eggs Monique

Shenandoah Growers, Inc.—Harrisonburg

1 tsp. + 3 Tbsp. BUTTER
12 MUSHROOMS, sliced
2 Tbsp. minced fresh SHENANDOAH GROWERS® PARSLEY
1 clove GARLIC, minced
3 Tbsp. FLOUR
2 tsp. minced fresh SHENANDOAH GROWERS® DILL
1 1/2 cups MILK
2 cups 1-inch pieces ASPARAGUS, cooked until tender
6 HARD-BOILED EGGS, sliced
1 cup shredded MONTEREY JACK CHEESE
5 slices BACON, cooked and crumbled
2 Tbsp. soft BREAD CRUMBS

In a small saucepan, melt 1 teaspoon butter; add mushrooms and cook until tender. Stir in parsley and set aside. In a medium saucepan, melt remaining butter; stir in garlic, flour and dill. Add milk and cook, stirring constantly, until mixture starts to boil. Stir in asparagus and remove from heat. Butter a round, 8-inch baking dish; spoon in half of the sauce mixture. Top with egg slices, mushrooms and remaining asparagus sauce. Sprinkle with cheese, bacon and bread crumbs. Bake at 350° for 15 minutes.

Serves 4.

Eggs à la Jefferson

"One cannot live so close to Monticello, the home of Thomas Jefferson and not have a signature dish named for him."

Rebecca Lindway—The Inn at Monticello, Charlottesville

16 EGGS
SALT and PEPPER to taste
10 strips of BACON, cooked and crumbled
Fresh MUSHROOMS, sliced
1 1/2 cups CHEDDAR CHEESE, shredded
1/2 cup SOUR CREAM
4 GREEN ONIONS, chopped
TOMATOES, thinly sliced

Scramble eggs to soft scramble (do not overcook!). Place eggs as first layer in a 9 x 13 baking dish that has been sprayed with cooking spray. Top with salt and pepper, bacon, mushrooms, cheese, and dollops of sour cream. Sprinkle with green onions. Cover and place in refrigerator if not using immediately. If refrigerated, bring to room temperature before cooking. Heat oven to 350° and bake for 20 to 25 minutes, or until heated through and cheese is bubbly. Place each serving on platters and garnish with tomato slices.

Serves 10.

Thomas Jefferson

The 3rd president of the United States (1801-1809), Thomas Jefferson is best remembered as the author of the Declaration of Independence and founder of the Democratic party. He was also a multi-talented inventor and writer and became the foremost American architect of his time. He designed the Virginia Capitol, the University of Virginia and his own home, Monticello, which stands on top of a mountain near Charlottesville. (See photo back cover)

Virginia Ham & Broccoli O'Brien

"This dish has become a favorite family tradition to serve at our annual pre-Thanksgiving brunch. It is especially wonderful to serve to guests to provide Southern hospitality!"

Debra W. Pershing—Hopewell

10-12 slices WHITE BREAD, buttered
2 cups diced baked VIRGINIA HAM
1 pkg. (10 oz.) frozen chopped BROCCOLI, cooked
1 pkg. (24 oz.) frozen HASH BROWN POTATOES O'BRIEN,
    thawed
1/2 cup chopped ONION
3 cups shredded SHARP CHEDDAR CHEESE
6 EGGS, slightly beaten
2-2 1/2 cups HALF AND HALF
1/4 tsp. DIJON MUSTARD
SALT and PEPPER to taste

In an 8 x 12 baking dish, layer in order: bread, ham, broccoli, potatoes and onion. Top with cheese. In a medium mixing bowl, combine eggs, half and half, mustard, salt and pepper; mix well. Pour over top of cheese. Cover and refrigerate 8 hours or overnight. Remove from refrigerator, let stand for 30 minutes and then bake, uncovered, at 325° for 1 hour.

Serves 6-8.

Crabmeat Quiche

8 oz. SWISS CHEESE,
    finely shredded
2 Tbsp. FLOUR
2 EGGS, beaten
1/2 cup MILK
1/2 cup MAYONNAISE

4 GREEN ONIONS, chopped
1 lb. CRABMEAT
SALT and PEPPER to taste
1 (9-inch) unbaked DEEP DISH
    PIE SHELL

In a large bowl, combine all ingredients . Pour mixture into pie shell and bake at 350° for 45 minutes.

Serves 4.

Raspberry-Stuffed French Toast With Blackberry Syrup

A lower fat version of French toast, this dish is baked instead of fried.

Developed for Millcroft Farms Co. by Janice Therese Mancuso

2 oz. NEUFCHÂTEL CHEESE, softened
1/2 cup FAT FREE SOUR CREAM
1/4 cup SUGAR
1/4 tsp. LEMON EXTRACT
3 EGGS
1/4 cup HALF AND HALF
3/4 cup WATER
16 slices FRENCH BREAD
1 cup RASPBERRIES
2 Tbsp. MILLCROFT FARMS COMPANY® BLACKBERRY SYRUP

In a small bowl, blend Neufchâtel cheese, sour cream, sugar and lemon extract. Set aside. In a glass measuring cup, whisk eggs with half and half and water. Pour 1/2 of the egg mixture into a buttered casserole dish. Place 8 slices of bread in casserole dish. Spread cheese mixture evenly over bread. Sprinkle with raspberries and drizzle with blackberry syrup. Top with remaining bread and pour remaining egg mixture over top. Bake in a preheated 350° oven for 20 minutes. Cool slightly before serving. Can be made ahead and heated in a microwave oven.

Serves 4.

Blue Ridge Parkway

The Blue Ridge Parkway is a 469-mile scenic road that follows the crest of the Blue Ridge Mountains. It connects Shenandoah National Park in Virginia and the Great Smoky Mountains National Park in North Carolina and Tennessee.

Pernie's Chocolate Gravy

"My sister, Pernie, made this for us on weekends as we were growing up—it was our favorite!"

Bea Golden—Tappahannock

2 Tbsp. COCOA	2 1/2 cups MILK
3 heaping Tbsp. FLOUR	1 Tbsp. VANILLA
1 1/4 cups SUGAR	1/2 stick BUTTER or
1/2 tsp. SALT	MARGARINE

Mix dry ingredients together in a skillet. Add just enough milk to make a thin paste, then add the remainder of milk and the vanilla. Cook over low heat, stirring constantly, until mixture has thickened to the consistency of gravy. Remove from heat and add dollops of butter on top.

Note: Can be served over biscuits, pancakes, waffles, pound cake or just about anything that you want to add a sweet topping to.

Elizabeth's Baked Bananas

"I developed this recipe to serve with muffins. It's very easy, doesn't take much time to prepare and delicious. It's also my most requested recipe."

Elizabeth McKenry-Adams—Nana's Cottage Bed & Breakfast, Lynchburg

1 BANANA
2 tsp. BROWN SUGAR
2 tsp. BUTTER or MARGARINE, melted
1 cup SPECIAL K® or CORN FLAKES

Cut banana in half, then slice lengthwise. Place bananas in a baking dish (or two individual baking dishes) and sprinkle with brown sugar. Stir butter into cereal. Spoon over banana slices. Bake at 350° for 10 minutes.

Serves 2.

Ann's Coffee Cake

"This recipe is a favorite of our family. My heritage dates back to the Old German Baptist Brethren, who left Germany in pursuit of religious freedom in the 1700s."

Ann Hubbard DeMaury—Ann's Apple Butter, Troutville

1 1/2 cups SUGAR	1 Tbsp. BAKING POWDER
1/2 cup MARGARINE, softened	1 tsp. SALT
2 EGGS, beaten	1 cup MILK
3 cups FLOUR	1 tsp. VANILLA

In a large bowl, mix sugar, margarine and eggs. In another bowl, sift flour, baking powder and salt together and add to egg mixture alternating with milk and vanilla. Spread half of the batter in a greased 9 x 13 pan. Spread half of the ***Brown Sugar & Coconut Topping*** over batter in pan and swirl with a fork for a marbled effect. Add remaining batter and topping, swirling again. Bake at 350° for 30-40 minutes or until center springs back when lightly touched with fingertips.

Brown Sugar & Coconut Topping

1 cup packed BROWN SUGAR	1/4 cup WATER
1/4 cup FLOUR	1 cup COCONUT FLAKES or
1/4 cup BUTTER, melted	chopped NUTS
4 tsp. CINNAMON	

In a medium bowl, mix topping ingredients.

Roanoke

Roanoke, called the "Capital of the Blue Ridge," lies on the Roanoke River and is nestled between the Blue Ridge and Allegheny Mountains. It is one of Virginia's largest cities and an industrial railroad and convention center. In 1881, Roanoke was a small pioneer settlement called Big Lick, named after a large salt marsh where deer fed. In 1882, two railways made a junction at Big Lick. The town was renamed Roanoke in 1882.

Bauernfrühstück
(German Farmer's Breakfast)

*"This is a family favorite. I sometimes make it using Ore-Ida's®
Potatoes O'Brien, a frozen food product that has the potatoes,
peppers and onions already in it."*

Madge Quadros—Newport News

6 slices BACON
1 sm. GREEN BELL PEPPER, diced
2 Tbsp. finely chopped ONION
3 lg. POTATOES, boiled, peeled and cubed
SALT and PEPPER to taste
1/2 cup grated CHEDDAR CHEESE
6 EGGS

In a skillet, fry bacon until light brown and crisp. Drain on
paper towels; crumble when cool. Drain off all but 3 tablespoons
of the bacon drippings and add green pepper, onion, potatoes,
salt and pepper. Cook over medium heat until potatoes are
golden, stirring frequently. Sprinkle cheese over potatoes and
stir. Break eggs into pan over potatoes, stir in bacon and cook
over low heat, stirring constantly, until eggs are set.

Serves 6.

Apple Butter-Walnut Pancakes

Serve these moist, flavorful pancakes with apple syrup.

Developed for Ann's Apple Butter by Janice Therese Mancuso

2 EGGS, slightly beaten
1 cup YOGURT
1/2 cup ANN'S® APPLE BUTTER

1 1/2 cups FLOUR
2 tsp. BAKING POWDER
1/2 cup chopped WALNUTS

In a large bowl, whisk eggs, yogurt and apple butter. Add
flour, baking powder and walnuts. Batter will be thick. For a
thinner batter, stir in a small amount of water. Cook on a hot,
greased griddle, turning to brown both sides.

Makes 8 pancakes.

Orange French Toast

"We sometimes have guests who have allergies to milk. This recipe uses orange juice instead of milk, and our guests love it!"

Rebecca Lindway—The Inn at Monticello, Charlottesville

4 oz. BUTTER
1/2 cup packed BROWN SUGAR
CINNAMON to taste
Dried ORANGE PEEL
7 lg. EGGS
1 1/2 cups ORANGE JUICE
10 thick slices BREAD, crusts removed

3 ORANGES
1 pint STRAWBERRIES
1/6 lg. MUSKMELON
4 lg. PEACHES
1/2 cup SUGAR
1/4 cup TRIPLE SEC

Melt butter in a 10 x 15 glass baking dish; sprinkle with brown sugar, cinnamon and orange peel. In a large bowl, beat eggs; stir in orange juice. Dip bread slices in egg mixture and place in baking dish. Bake in a 350° oven for 40 minutes. Meanwhile, slice fruits and place in a large bowl. Add sugar and Triple Sec; stir to blend. Let fruit mixture set for 1/2 hour. To serve, place French toast upside down on plates; top with fruit.

Serves 10.

Apple Pie Breakfast Casserole

"We use this recipe at our school breakfast once a month."

Bettie P. Shelton—Petersburg

1 lb. BACON or BULK SAUSAGE, cooked
1 (9-inch) unbaked DEEP DISH PIE SHELL
1 lg. can (21 oz.) APPLE PIE FILLING
1/2 cup shredded SHARP CHEDDAR CHEESE

Crumble bacon or sausage into the pie shell. Gently spread pie filling over meat. Bake at 350° for 15 minutes; sprinkle cheese on top and continue to bake 10 minutes longer or until cheese is melted.

Serves 6.

Mulligatawny Soup

Originally an Indian dish, this soup was adapted by the British. It is believed to be one of Thomas Jefferson's favorite meals.

2 Tbsp. BUTTER	1/2 cup uncooked WHITE RICE
1/2 cup chopped ONION	1 Tbsp. CURRY POWDER
1 lg. CARROT, chopped	1/2 tsp. THYME
1 stalk CELERY, chopped	1/2 tsp. PEPPER
1 APPLE, peeled and diced	2 cups cooked, cubed CHICKEN
3 cups CHICKEN BROTH	1/4 cup chopped fresh PARSLEY
1 cup WATER	1/2 cup HEAVY CREAM

Melt butter in a large saucepan. Add onion, carrot, celery and apple. Cook for 10 minutes, stirring occasionally. Add broth, water, rice, curry powder, thyme and pepper. Bring to a boil. Reduce heat and simmer, covered, for 20 minutes or until rice is cooked. Stir in chicken and parsley. Cover and simmer for 5 minutes or until very hot. Remove from heat and stir in cream. Serve immediately.

Serves 4.

Bacon-Corn Chowder

1 lb. BACON
2 cans (17 oz. ea.) CREAMED CORN
3 cups MILK
2 cups shredded SHARP CHEDDAR CHEESE
1/2 cup chopped GREEN ONIONS
1 tsp. PEPPER

In a large saucepan, fry bacon until crisp. Drain, cool and crumble. Pour drippings out of saucepan; add corn and milk. Cook over medium heat until mixture starts to bubble. Add cheese, green onions, bacon and pepper and bring to a boil.

Serves 6.

Virginia's Atlantic Coastal Plain

A lowland region about 100 miles wide extends north and south along the eastern coast of the state and is sometimes called the Tidewater, because tidal water flows up its bays, inlets and rivers. Chesapeake Bay divides the region into a western section and a peninsula called the Eastern Shore. The region has many salt marshes and swamps. The largest of these, Dismal Swamp, is in the southeast.

Seafood Chowder

This chowder uses a combination of fresh Virginia seafoods.

6 slices BACON
1 lg. ONION, chopped
3 lg. POTATOES, chopped
2 1/2 cups WATER
2 cups HALF AND HALF

1 lb. COD or FLOUNDER
   FILLETS
1/2 lb. SHRIMP
1 can (6 oz.) CRABMEAT

In a skillet, cook bacon until crisp; drain, cool and crumble. Cook onion in bacon drippings. Set aside. In a large saucepan, cook potatoes in water and half and half until tender, about 15 minutes. Add seafood and cook 10 minutes. Stir in bacon and onions. Cook 5 minutes, stirring occasionally. Do not boil.

Serves 6.

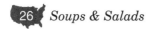

Gazpacho

An adaptation of a recipe served at colonial Williamsburg.

1 lg. CUCUMBER, peeled, chopped
1/2 RED ONION, peeled, chopped
1/2 GREEN BELL PEPPER, seeded, chopped
1 stalk CELERY, chopped
2 cloves GARLIC, peeled
1 cup SOFT BREAD CRUMBS (large pieces)
4 lg. RIPE TOMATOES, peeled and seeded
2 cups TOMATO JUICE
1/2 cup WINE
1 Tbsp. OLIVE OIL
2 tsp. LEMON JUICE
Freshly ground BLACK PEPPER to taste
CROUTONS or chopped HARD-BOILED EGG for garnish

Place first six ingredients in the bowl of a food processor. Use pulse motion to chop fine. Add remaining ingredients (except croutons or egg) and process to desired consistency. Add garnish just before serving.

Serves 4.

Roma's Garden Fresh Soup

"My mother, Roma, only used fresh vegetables from her garden or those that she had canned."

Shelby J. (Adkins) Barton—Haysi

2 lbs. GROUND BEEF
2 qts. WATER
2-3 qts. canned TOMATOES
2 cups diced CARROTS
1 head CABBAGE, diced
1 lg. ONION, diced
4 cups diced POTATOES
SALT and PEPPER to taste
1 box (16 oz.) ELBOW
   MACARONI

In a large skillet, brown beef; drain. Place beef in a large soup pot; add water and tomatoes. Heat to simmering; add carrots, cabbage, onion, potatoes, salt and pepper. Cook slowly for 3-4 hours. Add a small amount of tomato juice if necessary. Prepare macaroni according to the directions; drain. Spoon over macaroni in soup bowls. Serve with cornbread.

The Best Seafood Gumbo

*"This recipe was given to me by a friend who's uncle
was an 'oyster man' from Louisiana."*

Patricia Henderson—Prince George

6 Tbsp. BACON DRIPPINGS
6 Tbsp. FLOUR
1 cup chopped ONION
1 cup chopped CELERY
1 cup chopped GREEN ONIONS
2 cloves GARLIC, minced
1/2 lb. OKRA, chopped
1 can (16 oz.) TOMATOES, chopped
4 cups CHICKEN BROTH
1/2 cup chopped fresh PARSLEY
4 cups WATER
2 BAY LEAVES
1/2 tsp. THYME
1/2 tsp. BASIL
CAYENNE to taste
SALT and PEPPER to taste
HOT SAUCE to taste
2 lbs. SHRIMP, shelled and deveined
1 pt. OYSTERS
1 lb. LUMP CRABMEAT
Cooked RICE

In a heavy stock pot, heat bacon drippings over medium heat. Stir in flour and cook until rich brown in color. Add onion, celery, green onions and garlic. Cook 10-12 minutes, stirring constantly, until vegetables are wilted. In a small skillet, cook okra in oil until tender. Add okra, tomatoes, broth, parsley, water, bay leaves and seasonings to the onion mixture; simmer slowly for 10 minutes. Remove from heat and refrigerate overnight. When reheating, remove bay leaves and add shrimp, oysters and crabmeat; heat for 10-15 minutes. Serve hot over rice.

Serves 6-8.

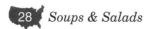

Red Brunswick Stew

"This is just delicious. A shortcut version of the classic Southern stew. Enjoy!"

Martha Ann Richards—Newport News

3 slices BACON, cut in half
1 can (16 oz.) STEWED TOMATOES
1 can (15 oz.) POTATOES, drained
1 pkg. (10 oz.) frozen SUCCOTASH, thawed
1 can (14.5 oz.) CHICKEN BROTH
1 can (6 oz.) TOMATO JUICE
1/4 cup chopped ONION
SALT and PEPPER to taste
1/4 cup COLD WATER
2 Tbsp. ALL-PURPOSE FLOUR
2 cups cubed cooked CHICKEN

In a large saucepan, cook bacon until crisp; remove and drain on paper towels. Drain drippings from skillet, add tomatoes, potatoes, succotash, chicken broth, tomato juice, onion, salt and pepper. Bring to a boil, then reduce heat, cover and simmer for 15-20 minutes. In a small bowl, combine water and flour, stirring until smooth; stir into tomato mixture. Cook and stir until mixture has thickened. Stir in chicken. Cook on low heat for an additional 10-15 minutes. Spoon into bowls and top with crumbled bacon.

Serves 4.

Broccoli Salad

3 cups diced BROCCOLI
1/2 cup diced GREEN ONIONS
2 HARD-BOILED EGGS, chopped

1/2 cup chopped WALNUTS
1/2 cup MAYONNAISE
SALT and PEPPER to taste

Mix broccoli, green onions, eggs and walnuts in a large bowl. Stir in mayonnaise; add salt and pepper. Refrigerate until ready to serve.

Serves 8.

Lamb & Fennel Salad

"This salad is so good and nutritious, too! The goat cheese is from a local cheesemaker, Rucker Farm in Flint Hill. Our winery serves local cheeses with our wines."

Nancy Law—Linden Vineyards, Linden

20 sm. slices rare-cooked, cold LAMB
4 oz. RUCKER FARM® GOAT CHEESE, crumbled
2 cups sliced fresh FENNEL
Chopped FENNEL FRONDS, to taste
3/4 cup SALAD OIL
1/4 cup WHITE WINE VINEGAR
1 tsp. crumbled ROSEMARY
1/2 tsp. SALT
1 Tbsp. APRICOT PRESERVES

In a medium mixing bowl, combine lamb, cheese, fennel and fronds; chill. In a salad dressing bottle, combine oil, vinegar, rosemary, salt and preserves; shake until thick. Let stand at room temperature for several hours. Shake again and serve over chilled salad. Serve with Seyval or Sauvignon Blanc wine.

Serves 4.

Macaroni & Cheese Salad

Meryl Bernstein—Richmond

1 1/2 cups MAYONNAISE
2/3 cup MILK
3 Tbsp. fresh DILL
SALT and PEPPER to taste
1 box (16 oz.) LARGE SHELL PASTA, cooked
1 1/2 lbs. sharp CHEDDAR CHEESE, cubed
1 bunch RADISHES, sliced
2 med. GREEN BELL PEPPERS, sliced

In a large bowl, combine mayonnaise, milk, dill, salt and pepper. Fold in remaining ingredients. Cover and refrigerate until ready to serve.

Marinated Vegetable Salad

*"This salad is a delicious and beautiful way to serve
Virginia's market-fresh vegetables."*

Gina Reed—Mrs. Gina's Herbs & Things, Roanoke

Marinade:
**1/2 cup MRS. GINA'S® DILL
HERBAL VINEGAR
1 cup OIL
1 Tbsp. ACCENT®**

**1 Tbsp. GARLIC SALT
1 Tbsp. SALT
1 1/2 tsp. PEPPER**

**1 head CAULIFLOWER, chopped
1 bunch BROCCOLI, chopped
1 lb. MUSHROOMS, whole or sliced
1 can (2.25 oz.) diced BLACK OLIVES
3 cups sliced CARROTS
1 basket CHERRY TOMATOES, stemmed**

In a small bowl, combine marinade ingredients. Place vegetables in a large glass or ceramic bowl, add marinade and toss. Marinate in refrigerator for 24 hours, stirring several times.

Blackberry-Thyme Vinaigrette

Try this sweet yet savory dressing on red leaf lettuce with goat cheese and toasted walnuts.

Developed for Millcroft Farms Co. by Janice Therese Mancuso

**1/2 cup MILLCROFT FARMS COMPANY® BLACKBERRY SYRUP
1/4 cup RICE VINEGAR
3 Tbsp. OLIVE OIL
2 Tbsp. finely chopped GREEN ONIONS
1 tsp. finely chopped fresh THYME**

Mix all ingredients in a small bottle (top with cap and shake well), or in a glass measuring cup (mix well with a fork). May be stored in refrigerator for 2 weeks. Shake or stir well before serving.

Makes about 1 cup.

Black-eyed Pea Salad

Carol Austin—Sutherlin

3 cans (15 oz. ea.) BLACK-EYED PEAS
1 1/2 cups APPLE CIDER VINEGAR
Pinch SALT
PEPPER, to taste
1 1/2 cups HONEY
1/2 cup each chopped GREEN, RED and YELLOW BELL PEPPER
1/4 cup chopped ONION (optional)

Pour peas into a colander, rinse well and drain thoroughly. In a large bowl, mix vinegar, salt, pepper and honey with a wire whisk until well-blended. Add peppers, onions and peas. Mix well; refrigerate. Toss with ***Honey Sauce*** just before serving.

Serves 8 to 10.

Honey Sauce

1 cup HONEY   **1/2 cup KETCHUP**
1/4 cup VINEGAR   **1/4 cup MUSTARD**

Mix all ingredients well.

Ginger Honey Salad Dressing

Virginia State Beekeepers Association—Glen Allen

1/2 cup VEGETABLE OIL
1/2 cup RICE WINE VINEGAR
1/4 cup HONEY
3 Tbsp. toasted SESAME SEEDS
3/4 tsp. SESAME OIL
2 Tbsp. grated fresh GINGERROOT
1 clove GARLIC, minced
1/8 tsp. crushed RED PEPPER FLAKES
SALT to taste

In a small bowl, whisk ingredients together thoroughly. Chill until ready to toss with your favorite salad.

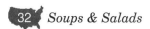

Minted Chicken Salad

"This recipe is 'as Southern as a mint julep!' Mint grows abundantly here and this original recipe is a favorite with our customers. Try it on a hot summer day."

Richard R. Hanson—Rebec Vineyards, Amherst

1 whole CHICKEN
Dressing:
   3/4 cup MAYONNAISE
   3/4 cup plain YOGURT
   1/2 cup fresh MINT
1 cup seedless GRAPES
1/2 cup slivered ALMONDS
1 head RED LEAF or RED ROMAINE LETTUCE

In a large pot, poach chicken for 45 minutes or until done. Combine dressing ingredients, cover and chill. Debone the chicken; cut into bite-size pieces and place in a bowl. Add grapes and almonds; toss to mix well. Pour dressing over the chicken mixture; cover and chill for at least 1 hour. Serve on a bed of lettuce, garnished with fresh fruit slices and sprigs of mint. This is especially good if served with a blush wine.

Rowena's Potato Salad

Rowena's, Inc.—Norfolk

2 lbs. RED POTATOES
1/4 lb. BACON
1/4 cup chopped GREEN ONION
1/2 cup chopped CELERY
1/3 cup chopped fresh PARSLEY

1/3 cup MAYONNAISE
1 Tbsp. WHITE WINE VINEGAR
4 Tbsp. ROWENA'S® DEVILISH
   MUSTARD SAUCE
SALT and PEPPER to taste

Cook potatoes in salted water until tender; let cool then dice and place in a large bowl. In a skillet, cook bacon, drain on paper towels and crumble. Add bacon, green onion, celery and parsley to potatoes; mix well. In a small bowl, combine 2 tablespoons bacon drippings, mayonnaise, vinegar and mustard sauce. Toss with potato mixture, adding salt and pepper to taste.

Serves 6.

Pasta Salad

"This recipe is a crowd pleaser. It's perfect for family reunions and summer cookouts."

Gina Reed—Mrs. Gina's Herbs & Things, Roanoke

8 oz. SPIRAL PASTA, cooked and drained

Marinade:
   1 cup SALAD OIL
   1 cup MRS. GINA'S® GARLIC LOVER'S DELIGHT
      HERBAL VINEGAR
   1 cup SUGAR

1 cup shredded CARROTS
1 cup chopped CELERY
1 cup shredded MOZZARELLA CHEESE
1 cup shredded COLBY CHEESE
3 TOMATOES, chopped
2 CUCUMBERS, chopped

Cook pasta according to package directions. Mix marinade ingredients together and pour over hot pasta. Refrigerate pasta mixture overnight. When ready to serve, fold in remaining ingredients.

Salmon Salad

Min Bernstein—Richmond

3 AVOCADOS
LETTUCE
1 can (15 oz.) SALMON, chilled

2 Tbsp. sliced GREEN ONION
2 Tbsp. sliced CELERY

Dressing:
   1/3 cup OIL
   1 1/2 Tbsp. LEMON JUICE
   1 sm. clove GARLIC, minced

   1/8 tsp. DRY MUSTARD
   SALT and PEPPER to taste
   1 1/2 tsp. minced PARSLEY

Halve, pit and peel avocados. Arrange on a bed of lettuce on salad plates. Drain salmon and separate into chunks. Place salmon in a bowl and toss lightly with green onion and celery. Fill avocado halves with salmon mixture. Combine dressing ingredients in a jar with a tight fitting lid and shake vigorously. Drizzle dressing over top of salmon mixture.

Main Dishes

Creamed Oysters with Virginia Ham

"A winning combination of two Virginia classics."

Sandra D. Crocker—S. Wallace Edwards & Sons, Inc., Surry

3 doz. (or 1 qt.) OYSTERS
1/4 cup BUTTER
1/4 cup FLOUR
2 cups CREAM
1/2 cup MILK
1/4 cup SHERRY
1/4 tsp. SALT
1/4 tsp. PEPPER
1 lb. EDWARDS'® VIRGINIA HAM, cooked and cubed
6 slices BREAD, toasted and cut into triangles

Cook and drain oysters, reserving 1 cup of liquid. In a large saucepan, melt butter. Stir in flour until well-blended. Add cream, oyster liquid, milk, sherry, salt and pepper. Stir until smooth and slightly thick. Add oysters and ham. Serve on toast points.

Serves 6.

Braised Salmon & Herbs

*This combination of fresh herbs really
complements the salmon.*

Shenandoah Growers, Inc.—Harrisonburg

2 lg. ONIONS, chopped
3 CARROTS, chopped
2 stalks CELERY, chopped
6 Tbsp. VIRGIN OLIVE OIL
3 fresh SHENANDOAH GROWERS® BAY LEAVES
3 sprigs fresh SHENANDOAH GROWERS® PARSLEY
2 Tbsp. minced, fresh SHENANDOAH GROWERS® DILL
1/2 cup WATER
7 lbs. SALMON
1 1/2 cups WHITE WINE

Preheat oven to 350°. In a medium saucepan, sauté onions,
carrots and celery in olive oil. In a small saucepan bring bay
leaves, parsley and dill to a boil in 1/2 cup water. Place salmon
in baking pan and top with both mixtures. Pour wine over all.
Cover and cook for 30 minutes.

Serves 8.

Turkey Casserole

*"Virginia is one of this country's leading turkey producers!
Served with a salad and fresh fruit, this makes a great meal!"*

Ann Hart—Bedford

1 pkg. (6 oz.) TURKEY STUFFING MIX
1/4 lb. MARGARINE, melted
4-5 cups shredded cooked TURKEY
1 can (10.75 oz.) CREAM OF CELERY SOUP
1 can (10.75 oz.) CREAM OF CHICKEN SOUP
1 can (14.5 oz.) CHICKEN BROTH

Combine stuffing mix and margarine; mix well. In a 13 x 9
casserole dish, place 1/2 of the stuffing mixture and then layer
with 1/2 of the turkey. Combine 1/2 of the broth with the celery
soup and pour over turkey. Layer remaining turkey. Mix balance
of broth with the chicken soup and pour over turkey. Top with
remaining stuffing mixture. Bake at 350° for 45-60 minutes.

Deviled Crabs

"A popular Eastern Shore recipe."

Myrtle Soles—Seaford

1 lb. CRABMEAT
1/2 cup RITZ® CRACKER CRUMBS
2 Tbsp. WORCESTERSHIRE SAUCE
1 Tbsp. PARSLEY FLAKES
1 Tbsp. CELERY SEEDS
2 EGGS, beaten

4 Tbsp. MAYONNAISE
2 Tbsp. MUSTARD
1/4 cup BUTTER, melted
Dash of HOT SAUCE
PAPRIKA

In a large bowl mix all ingredients except paprika, until well-blended. Spoon into oven-proof serving dishes or shells and sprinkle with paprika. Bake 1 hour at 350°. Serve hot.

Richmond

In 1609 Capt. John Smith founded a settlement he called "None Such." The city of Richmond which developed near there became the state capital in 1779. From 1861-1865, Richmond was the capital of the Confederate States of America. Almost totally destroyed at the end of the war, Richmond is now a major commercial, cultural, educational and historical center.

Unstuffed Peppers

Madeline Cales—S. Wallace Edwards & Sons, Inc., Surry

1/2 lb. GROUND BEEF
1 GREEN BELL PEPPER,
    cut in strips
1 cup cooked RICE
4 oz. KRAFT® CHEEZ WHIZ

1/2 cup chopped TOMATO
2 Tbsp. chopped ONION
SALT and PEPPER to taste
BASIL LEAVES to taste

In a skillet, brown beef and sauté bell peppers, drain. Add remaining ingredients and cook for 5 minutes.

Serves 2.

Blue Ridge Blues Meatloaf

*"From the heart of the Blue Ridge comes a sauce all its own—
a blend of tomatoes, molasses, bourbon and spices."*

William Barnhardt—Willaby's Fine Sauces, White Stone

2 lbs. GROUND BEEF or PORK
6 oz. WILLABY'S® BLUE RIDGE BLUES SAUCE
3 EGGS, beaten
1 1/4 cups ITALIAN BREAD CRUMBS
1/2 GREEN BELL PEPPER, chopped
2 Tbsp. chopped ONION

In a large bowl, mix all ingredients. Form into a loaf; place
in a greased loaf pan. Bake at 350° for 1 hour and 10 minutes;
remove from oven and drain. Spread top with additional sauce
and bake for another 20 minutes.

Serves 4.

HAMburgers

Rowena's, Inc.—Norfolk

1 lb. BAKED HAM, finely minced
1 EGG
1 Tbsp. chopped ONION
1/4 cup BREAD CRUMBS
3 Tbsp. ROWENA'S® DEVILISH
   MUSTARD SAUCE

1 Tbsp. MAYONNAISE
OLIVE OIL
4 ROLLS or BUNS
CHEESE, sliced
LETTUCE LEAVES
Sliced TOMATO

Combine the first six ingredients in a large bowl. Shape into
patties. Heat a small amount of oil in a skillet and cook patties
over medium heat for 5 minutes per side. Split rolls or buns and
place patties on bottom half. Layer with cheese, lettuce and
tomato and add top. Serve with a basket of **POTATO CHIPS.**

Serves 4.

Virginia Baked Country Ham

"My grandfather butchered his own hogs. After curing the meat for months, this was the best and easiest way to cook the hams."

Betty Fitzgerald—Lyndhurst

1 whole COUNTRY HAM
6-7 cups WATER

Preheat oven to 500°. In a small roaster, place ham in water and cook for 20 minutes at 500°. Turn off oven for 3 hours. Turn oven on again at 500° and cook for 20 minutes. Turn oven off and leave ham in oven overnight. Do not open oven during this entire time! Next morning, trim fat, baste with your favorite glaze and serve.

"Give Me Liberty or Give Me Death!"

Demanded Patrick Henry, in his famous speech at St. John's Church, Richmond, in 1775.

Welsh Rarebit

Early English settlers brought this recipe to Virginia.

1 1/2 cups MILK
1 Tbsp. DRY MUSTARD
2 cups grated SHARP CHEDDAR CHEESE
2 Tbsp. BUTTER
SALT and PEPPER to taste
8 slices BREAD, toasted

In a saucepan, heat milk and stir in mustard. Add cheese, 1/2 cup at a time, stirring to melt after each addition. Stir in butter, mixing until smooth. Add salt and pepper. Lay toast slices in a large baking dish (or individual baking dishes). Pour cheese mixture evenly over each slice. Broil until cheese is browned and bubbly. Serve immediately.

Serves 4.

My Garlic Heaven, a Chicken Thing

"Rebec Vineyards hosts the Annual Virginia Garlic Festival in October. This original recipe has captured the imagination of thousands of festival attendees."

Richard R. Hanson—Rebec Vineyards, Amherst

1 ROASTING CHICKEN
1 LEMON, halved
2 bulbs GARLIC, cloves separated
   and peeled
1 med. ONION, quartered
6 (3-inch) sprigs fresh ROSEMARY
   or 2 tsp. dried
1 cup WHITE WINE
CRACKED PEPPER to taste

Preheat oven to 350°. Place chicken in a roasting pan; rub chicken with the lemon then squeeze juice over all. Place 8 garlic cloves in the chicken's cavity and scatter the other cloves in pan. Place onion around the chicken. Stuff three rosemary sprigs in the chicken cavity. Snip the remaining rosemary and sprinkle over chicken and in the pan. Add wine and sprinkle chicken with pepper. Make a large tent of heavy aluminum foil and place it over top of roasting pan, sealing completely around edges. This will "steam" the chicken and allow for infusion of flavors. Bake for 15-20 minutes per pound of chicken. Let stand for 15 minutes before serving.

Booker T. Washington National Monument

This 224-acre monument, 30 miles southeast of Roanoke, preserves and protects the birthsite and childhood home of this internationally known African-American leader. Booker T. Washington graduated from Hampton Institute and received honorary degrees from both Harvard and Dartmouth.

Mom's Meatloaf

"I was raised on a small tobacco farm in the southwestern part of Virginia. My mother, Wilmetta Combs Latham, was a wonderful farm cook. There was not a lot of money, but our mama's cooking made us feel rich and loved."

Peggy Semancik—Abingdon

1/2 cup BREAD CRUMBS
1/4 cup MILK
1 1/2 lbs. GROUND CHUCK
1 lg. EGG, beaten
1/2 cup chopped ONION
1 Tbsp. WORCESTERSHIRE SAUCE
3 Tbsp. KETCHUP
1 Tbsp. MUSTARD
1/4 cup TOMATO SAUCE
1/2 tsp. SALT
1/2 tsp. PEPPER
1 Tbsp. finely chopped GREEN BELL PEPPER
2 rings GREEN BELL PEPPER

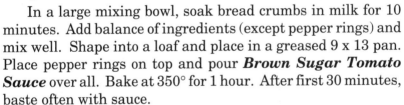

In a large mixing bowl, soak bread crumbs in milk for 10 minutes. Add balance of ingredients (except pepper rings) and mix well. Shape into a loaf and place in a greased 9 x 13 pan. Place pepper rings on top and pour ***Brown Sugar Tomato Sauce*** over all. Bake at 350° for 1 hour. After first 30 minutes, baste often with sauce.

Brown Sugar Tomato Sauce

1 1/4 cups TOMATO SAUCE   2 Tbsp. VINEGAR
2 Tbsp. BROWN SUGAR   1/4 cup WATER

Combine all sauce ingredients together and mix well.

Natural Bridge

One of America's most recognizable icons, this natural wonder is a sacred site to the Monacan Indians, a functioning bridge, a tourist destination and an ever popular artists' subject. The bridge is a limestone arch 250 feet high and 90 feet long.

Poppy Seed Chicken Casserole

"This recipe was given to me several years ago."

Dorothy T. Hunter—Bedford

2 sleeves KEEBLER® TOWNHOUSE CRACKERS, crumbled
2 sticks BUTTER or MARGARINE, melted
2 Tbsp. POPPY SEEDS
8-10 CHICKEN BREASTS, cooked and diced
2 cans (10.75 oz. ea.) CREAM OF CHICKEN SOUP
1 ctn. (16 oz.) LOW FAT SOUR CREAM (not fat-free)
1/4 cup CHICKEN BROTH

In a medium mixing bowl, mix crackers with butter and poppy seeds. Line a 9 x 13 glass pan with 2/3 of the cracker mixture. In a separate mixing bowl, mix chicken with soup, sour cream and chicken broth; blend well. Pour mixture over cracker layer. Sprinkle top with remaining cracker mixture. Bake at 350° for 1 hour. Serve over rice.

Crab Casserole

"The Chesapeake Bay is noted for its abundance and quality of blue crabs. In this recipe, Old Bay Seasoning is the secret spice that enhances the delicacy of the crabmeat."

Mary C. Haden—Hopewell

1 lb. LUMP CRABMEAT
3 Tbsp. MAYONNAISE
1 tsp. MUSTARD
1 tsp. OLD BAY SEASONING®
1 tsp. fresh or flaked PARSLEY
1 med. ONION, minced
1 EGG, slightly beaten
1/4 cup finely crushed CRACKERS
1/2 stick UNSALTED BUTTER
1 tsp. WORCESTERSHIRE SAUCE

In a large mixing bowl, blend all ingredients together. Pour into an ungreased 1-quart casserole dish and bake at 350° for 50-60 minutes or until top is golden brown.

Chicken, Polish Sausage & Ham Jambalaya

*"I won 2nd place in a local newspaper contest
with this recipe!"*

Marie Holdren Wagner—Bedford

3 Tbsp. UNSALTED BUTTER
1/2 lb. POLISH SAUSAGE, cut into 1/4-inch slices
1/2 lb. LEAN HAM, cubed
2 BAY LEAVES
1 Tbsp. POULTRY SEASONING
1 cup chopped ONION
1 cup chopped CELERY
1 cup chopped GREEN BELL PEPPER
1 Tbsp. minced GARLIC
1/2 cup TOMATO SAUCE
1 cup peeled, chopped TOMATOES
2 cups chunked, cooked CHICKEN BREAST
2 1/2 cups CHICKEN STOCK
1 1/2 cups uncooked CONVERTED RICE

In a 4-quart saucepan, melt butter over high heat. Add sausage and ham and cook for 4-5 minutes or until meat starts to brown. Stir frequently and scrape pan as needed. Stir in bay leaves, poultry seasoning, 1/2 cup each of onion, celery, bell pepper and the garlic. Stirring frequently, cook mixture 6-8 minutes or until vegetables begin to soften. Stir in tomato sauce and cook for 1 minute, stirring often. Add remaining onion, celery, bell pepper and the tomatoes. Stir in chicken, chicken stock and rice and mix well. Reduce heat; cover and simmer over very low heat for 30 minutes. Stir well and remove bay leaves; let set for 5 minutes before serving.

Serves 6.

Did You Know?

The Civil War ended when Confederate General Robert E. Lee surrendered to Union General Ulysses S. Grant at the Appomattox Court House—April 9, 1865.

Cajun Jambalaya

"An unusual variation of jambalaya and very tasty. It's a great dish for a big crowd!"

Elinor S. Wilson—Bunker Hill Foods, Bedford

1/3 cup BACON DRIPPINGS
4 cups chopped ONION
3 cups chopped CELERY
2 cups chopped GREEN BELL PEPPER
1 cup chopped SMOKED HAM
3 1/2 cups chopped SMOKED SAUSAGE
6 BAY LEAVES

1 can (28 oz.) WHOLE TOMATOES, undrained
1 cup TOMATO JUICE
1 1/4 oz. JAMBALAYA SEASONING
1/2 tsp. TABASCO®
3 1/2 cups uncooked RICE
4 cups CHICKEN BROTH

In a large skillet, heat bacon drippings over medium heat. Add onions, celery and bell pepper. Sauté for 20 minutes or until vegetables are tender. Add ham and sausage; cook for 8 minutes. Add bay leaves, tomatoes, tomato juice, jambalaya seasoning and Tabasco; cover and simmer for 15 minutes. Turn heat to high and stir in rice and chicken broth. Bring mixture to a boil, cover and simmer for 15 minutes or until rice has absorbed most of the liquid. Remove bay leaves and serve.

Makes 1 gallon.

Whiskey-Pepper Chops

Virginia Pork Producers—Richmond

1 Tbsp. MOLASSES
1/2 tsp. fresh LEMON JUICE
1/4 cup BUTTER, softened
1/3 cup WHISKEY
1/2 tsp. SALT

4 Tbsp. coarsely ground BLACK PEPPER
4 (1 1/4-inch thick) bone-in PORK CHOPS

In a small bowl, stir together the molasses, lemon juice and butter. Cover and refrigerate. In a shallow bowl, combine the whiskey and salt. Place the pepper in another shallow bowl. Dip both sides of each chop in the whiskey mixture, then evenly coat with pepper. Grill for 12 to 16 minutes, turning once, until just done. Top each chop with butter sauce and serve.

Blue Ribbon Lasagna

"My daughter, Deborah Hadden Reeves, entered this recipe at the Virginia State 4-H Congress and won a Blue Ribbon!"

Jacqueline M. Hadden—Lynchburg

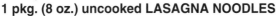

1 lb. GROUND BEEF
1/4 tsp. granulated GARLIC
1 can (8 oz.) TOMATO SAUCE
1 can (28 oz.) chopped TOMATOES
1/2 tsp. OREGANO
1/2 tsp. BASIL
1 tsp. SALT
1/4 tsp. PEPPER
1 sm. ONION, chopped
1 Tbsp. SALT
1 Tbsp. OIL
1 pkg. (8 oz.) uncooked LASAGNA NOODLES
1/2 lb. MUENSTER CHEESE, sliced
1 ctn. (12 oz.) COTTAGE CHEESE
1/3 cup grated PARMESAN CHEESE

Preheat oven to 375°. In a large skillet, brown beef and then drain off fat. Add garlic, tomato sauce, tomatoes, herbs, seasonings and onion to skillet and simmer for 20 minutes. Fill a large pot with water, stir in 1 tablespoon each of salt and oil and bring to a boil. Add noodles to pot and cook, uncovered, for 12 minutes. Drain. Arrange a layer of noodles in the bottom of a 2-quart casserole dish and layer 1/2 of the muenster cheese on top. Spread 1/2 of the cottage cheese on top of the muenster and 1/2 of the meat sauce on top of the cottage cheese. Repeat layers with remaining ingredients. Sprinkle top with Parmesan cheese and bake at 375° for 25-30 minutes.

Serves 4-6.

George Washington was born on a farm in Westmoreland County on February 22, 1732. He became the 1st President of the United States in 1789 and was re-elected in 1792.

Flowerdew Hundred Simple Pot Roast

"This recipe can be used for many kinds of meats such as beef, venison, etc."

Brenna Myers—Flowerdew Hundred Foundation, Hopewell

1 4-8 lb. ROAST	1 CABBAGE, sliced
1 sm. YELLOW ONION, sliced	1 tsp. SALT
Several YELLOW CARROTS (parsnips), scraped and sliced	1 tsp. PEPPER
	1 clove GARLIC, crushed
5-6 stalks CELERY, sliced	1 BAY LEAF
1 RUTABAGA, sliced	2 cups WATER

Place roast and vegetables in a large saucepan. Add spices and water. Bring to a boil, reduce to simmer and cook for 45 minutes.

Virginia Gourmet Croaker

Virginia Marine Products Board—Newport News

Marinade:

1/4 cup fresh LIME JUICE	1/4 tsp. NUTMEG
1/4 cup fresh LEMON JUICE	1/8 tsp. powdered GINGER
1/4 cup WHITE WINE	1/4 tsp. prepared
1/4 cup COOKING SHERRY	HORSERADISH
1/4 tsp. DILL	
4 (6-8-inch) CROAKER, heads removed	2 Tbsp. grated LEMON PEEL
	2 Tbsp. snipped fresh
SALT and PEPPER to taste	PARSLEY
1 cup clarified BUTTER	

Mix marinade ingredients. Score fish diagonally on both sides, three slits per side. Salt and pepper fish cavity and exterior. Place fish in a flat pan or casserole. Pour marinade over fish and marinate at least one hour, turning several times during process for even distribution. Remove fish and pat dry. Heat butter and brown fish until it flakes. Place fish on a warm serving platter. Add marinade to pan drippings and bring to a simmer. Add lemon peel and parsley; heat well and then pour over fish. Garnish with pimento, parsley and slices of lemon.

Side Dishes

Eastern Shore Fritters

"These recipes have been handed down at least four generations in my family. They are an Eastern Shore favorite. My grandmother told me that fritters were often made on fall mornings during harvest season, not only because of their wonderful flavor, but also because they went a long way and were inexpensive to make."

Tammy Belote Elvenia—Keller

Plain Pumpkin Fritters

3 cups PUMPKIN   1 1/2 cups FLOUR
1 3/4 cups SUGAR   2 Tbsp. VANILLA

In a large bowl, mix all ingredients until well blended. Drop carefully by spoonful into hot oil and cook until golden brown. Drain on paper towels.

Spicy Pumpkin Fritters

2 cups PUMPKIN   1/2 tsp. ALLSPICE
2 EGGS   1/2 tsp. VANILLA
1/2 cup SUGAR   FLOUR (approx. 1 cup)
1/2 tsp. CINNAMON

In a large bowl, combine all ingredients, adding just enough flour to make a thin batter. Test a small amount of batter in hot oil as you add flour. The thinner the fritter is, the better it will taste. Drop carefully by spoonful into hot oil and cook until golden brown. Drain on paper towels.

Zucchini Parmigiana

"The Italian influence in southwest Virginia comes from the immigrants who found work in the coal mines there."

Fran Hart—Bedford

2 Tbsp. OIL
1 Tbsp. BUTTER
1 lg. ZUCCHINI, sliced 1/2 inch thick
1 med. EGGPLANT, peeled and sliced
1 lg. ONION, coarsely chopped
1 tsp. ea. SALT and OREGANO
1/2 tsp. PEPPER
1 can (15 oz.) TOMATO SAUCE
1 lg. clove GARLIC, crushed
8 oz. MOZZARELLA CHEESE, sliced
2 Tbsp. grated PARMESAN CHEESE

In a large skillet over medium heat, melt butter; stir in oil. Add vegetables and cook for 10 minutes or until just tender; stir occasionally. Stir in salt, pepper and oregano. Spoon mixture into a greased 2-quart baking dish. Mix tomato sauce with garlic and pour over vegetables. Tuck cheese slices into vegetables so that about 1/2 of each slice is on the surface. Sprinkle with Parmesan cheese. Preheat oven to 375°. Bake casserole about 25 minutes, or until cheese is hot and bubbly.

Carrot Casserole

1/2 cup chopped ONION
4 Tbsp. BUTTER or MARGARINE
1/2 cup HALF AND HALF
1/2 cup ORANGE JUICE
1/2 tsp. NUTMEG
1/2 tsp. BLACK PEPPER
1 lb. CARROTS, chopped, cooked and mashed

In a small saucepan, sauté onion in 2 tablespoons butter until tender. Add remaining ingredients (except carrots) and combine. Blend onion mixture with carrots and mix thoroughly. Spoon into a greased casserole dish and dot top with butter. Bake at 350° for 20 minutes.

Serves 4.

Lillie Pearl's Sweet Potato Peach Surprise

"Lillie Pearl Fearnow, the creator of the well-known Virginia product, 'Mrs. Fearnow's Delicious Brunswick Stew with Chicken', treated her family often to this sweet potato and peach dish. It was always on her table at holiday times and is still a holiday must for her grandchildren and great-grandchildren. The business that Lillie Pearl started in her kitchen in the 1930's is still thriving over sixty years later."

Martha Fearnow—Mechanicsville

1 can (1 lb. 13 oz.) SWEET POTATOES, drained
2 Tbsp. BUTTER, melted
1 Tbsp. SUGAR
1/2 tsp. CINNAMON
1/4 tsp. NUTMEG
1/2 tsp. SALT
1 can (1lb. 13 oz.) PEACH HALVES, drained (reserve juice)
MARASCHINO CHERRIES

Blend sweet potatoes in a mixer until smooth. Blend in butter, sugar, cinnamon, nutmeg and salt. Place peach halves in baking dish with open halves up. Place a portion of the sweet potato mixture in each half. Pour cooled ***Peach Sauce*** over top of peaches. Top each serving with a maraschino cherry and bake at 300° for 15 minutes.

Peach Sauce

1 cup PEACH JUICE
1 cup packed LIGHT BROWN SUGAR
3 Tbsp. CORNSTARCH
2 Tbsp. fresh LEMON JUICE
1 Tbsp. grated LEMON RIND

Add enough water to reserved peach juice to make 1 cup. Pour into a saucepan and add brown sugar, cornstarch, lemon juice and rind. Cook until sauce thickens, stirring constantly. Set aside to cool.

Onion & Mushroom Casserole

1/2 lb. BACON
2 lg. ONIONS, coarsely chopped
1 lb. fresh MUSHROOMS, sliced
1 cup SOUR CREAM

2 EGGS, lightly beaten
1 cup shredded CHEDDAR
CHEESE

Cook bacon until crisp; drain, crumble and set aside. Sauté onions and mushrooms in bacon drippings until tender. In a bowl, stir sour cream into eggs. Add bacon, mushrooms, onions and half of the cheddar cheese. Pour mixture into a greased casserole dish. Sprinkle with remaining cheese. Bake at 375° for 30 minutes or until set.

Serves 4.

Jamestown

In May of 1607, three ships bringing 100 men sailed up the James River. The men landed and established the settlement they called Jamestown in honor of King James I of England. This was the first permanent English settlement in America.

Lilly's Beans

"I grew up loving country sausage. One day I decided to try adding it to my baked beans. My friends enjoy this recipe and I have shared it many times."

Lilly S. Chambers—Foster

1/3-1/2 lb. BULK PORK SAUSAGE
1/2 med. ONION, chopped
2 cans (16 oz. ea.) PORK and BEANS
6 Tbsp. BROWN SUGAR
4 Tbsp. KETCHUP

In a large skillet, brown sausage and onion. Set aside. Pour beans into a 2-quart casserole dish. Stir in brown sugar and ketchup, then add sausage mixture and stir. Bake at 350° for 30 minutes or microwave on high for 10 minutes.

Thurman's Hush Puppies

"This is our friend Thurman Johnson's special recipe
that he would serve at fish frys at his cabin on the lake."

Jane Bryan—Abingdon

1/2 cup SELF-RISING FLOUR	**1 lg. ONION, chopped**
1 cup SELF-RISING CORNMEAL	**1 EGG, beaten**
1/3 cup SUGAR	**MILK**

In a medium mixing bowl, combine flour, cornmeal, sugar, onion and egg. Add enough milk to make a thick dough. In a large skillet, heat oil. Carefully drop dough by spoonfuls into hot oil. Fry until golden brown on all sides. Drain on paper towels.

Fried Green Tomatoes

2 EGGS	**6 GREEN TOMATOES,**
3/4 cup CORNMEAL	**sliced 1/2 inch thick**
1/4 cup FLOUR	**BACON DRIPPINGS**

In a shallow bowl, beat eggs lightly. Blend cornmeal and flour in another shallow bowl. Coat tomato slices with egg mixture then the cornmeal mixture. Add bacon drippings to a skillet and fry tomatoes until both sides are golden brown.

Serves 4.

Creamy Sweet Potatoes

6 SWEET POTATOES
1/2 cup BUTTER, softened
1 cup packed BROWN SUGAR
1 tsp. CINNAMON

Bake potatoes in microwave or oven until tender; peel while still warm. Place potatoes in a large bowl and use a hand mixer to beat until smooth. Add butter, brown sugar and cinnamon. Beat with hand mixer again until creamy.

Serves 6.

Tomato Grunt

"This is a 1920s recipe handed down from my grandmother. We use Hanover tomatoes for this dish."

Pat Narron—Chester

3 lg. TOMATOES peeled, cored and chunked
4 BISCUITS or day-old **BREAD SLICES**, torn into pieces
1 cup packed BROWN SUGAR
1 stick BUTTER, cut into chunks

In a large mixing bowl, combine all ingredients. Pour mixture into a greased casserole dish. Bake at 350° for 45 minutes or until light brown on top.

Serves 4.

The Monitor and the Merrimack

Known as the "ironclads," the Monitor was originally built and covered with iron, while the Merrimack, renamed the Virginia, was a wooden ship that had been sunk, raised and covered with iron plates. Early in March of 1862 the two ships battled for four hours at Hampton Roads. Both ended the battle by withdrawing.

Cornbread Stuffing

This recipe will stuff a 10-pound turkey or it can be baked in a greased covered casserole dish at 325° for 45 minutes and served as a side dish.

1 1/2 cups CHICKEN BROTH   **6 cups CORNBREAD**, crumbled
1/2 cup sweet WHITE WINE   **1/2 tsp. THYME**
2 Tbsp. BUTTER or MARGARINE   **1/2 tsp. SAGE**
1 cup ONION, chopped   **1/2 tsp. BLACK PEPPER**
1/2 cup CELERY, chopped   **3 EGGS**, beaten

In a medium saucepan, bring chicken broth and wine to a simmer. Add butter; stir to melt. Add onion and celery and cook until tender, about 10 minutes. Set aside. In a large bowl, toss cornbread crumbs with thyme, sage and pepper. Add broth mixture and eggs. Mix well.

Broccoli Au Gratin

"My own recipe and a family favorite."

Mary Ann Wilson—Bristol

1 bunch BROCCOLI, chopped
1 1/2 cups MILK
2 Tbsp. FLOUR
2 Tbsp. MARGARINE

1/4 tsp. SALT
4 slices AMERICAN CHEESE,
cut into small pieces

Bring a large pot of water to boiling. Add broccoli, cover and reduce heat. Cook for 10-13 minutes or until broccoli is just tender; drain. In a medium saucepan, combine milk, flour, margarine and salt. Heat milk mixture slowly, then add American cheese and stir until melted. Place broccoli in a greased baking dish; pour the cheese sauce over top. Bake at 350° until sauce is bubbly.

Serves 4.

Mum-Mum's Corn Pudding Southern-Style

"This was my daughter-in-law's grandmother's recipe. It has been in her family for more than seventy-five years."

Marilyn Burnette—Gloucester

1/2 sleeve SALTINE CRACKERS,
crumbled
2 EGGS, beaten
1 can (15.25 oz.) CORN, drained
3 Tbsp. SUGAR

Pinch of SALT
1 1/2 tsp. VANILLA
1 1/2 tsp. NUTMEG
MILK
BUTTER

Preheat oven to 350°. In a medium mixing bowl, combine crackers, eggs, corn, sugar, salt, vanilla and nutmeg. Add enough milk to make mixture moderately soupy. Pour into a buttered 8 x 8 casserole dish; dot the top with butter. Bake at 350° for 25-30 minutes or until center is set.

Serves 4.

Grandma's Sweet Potato Pudding

"This has been a family recipe for over a century! I can remember my great-grandmother making this dish."

Barbara B. Pillow—Phenix

5 EGGS	**1 tsp. NUTMEG**
2 cups MILK	**1 tsp. CINNAMON**
2 cups SUGAR	**3 cups grated SWEET**
1 1/2 cups BUTTER, softened	**POTATOES**

In a large mixing bowl, beat eggs; add milk, sugar, butter and spices. Combine mixture with potatoes. Pour into a buttered casserole dish. Bake at 350° for 1 hour or until center is set.

Shenandoah National Park

Extending almost 105 miles along the crest of the Blue Ridge Mountains and with elevations ranging from 600 feet to 4,050 feet, Shenandoah National Park contains almost 197,000 acres of hiking trails and scenic viewpoints.

Clam Fritters

"This recipe came from my mother, Elizabeth Dukes. I have made these fritters for more than forty years."

Marian Thorowgood—Conway

20 CLAMS	**WATER**
2 EGGS, lightly beaten	**VEGETABLE OIL**
1 cup FLOUR	

Cook clams and reserve cooking liquid. Cut clams into small pieces. In a large bowl, combine eggs with flour. Add clams and enough reserved cooking liquids (diluted with water if too salty) to form a medium batter. Carefully drop spoonfuls of batter into hot vegetable oil in a skillet. Cook until golden brown. Drain well on paper towels before serving.

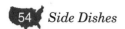

Sweet Potato Casserole

"My older sister gave me this recipe. It is a favorite at pot-luck church dinners."

Linda W. Ayers—Goodview

3 cups mashed SWEET POTATOES
1/2 cup SUGAR
1/2 cup packed BROWN SUGAR
2 EGGS, slightly beaten

1/2 cup MILK
1/2 stick BUTTER
1/2 tsp. SALT
1 tsp. VANILLA

Topping:
1 stick BUTTER
1 pkg. (7 oz.) shredded COCONUT
1 cup packed BROWN SUGAR
1/3 cup FLOUR

In a large mixing bowl, combine sweet potatoes, sugars, eggs, milk, butter, salt and vanilla; mix well. Pour into a buttered casserole dish. In a skillet, melt butter; add coconut, brown sugar and flour; stir well. Spread coconut mixture over potatoes. Bake at 350° for 30 minutes.

Marinated Vegetable Plate

"This is great for any get-together and travels well."

Fran Hart—Bedford

Marinade:
1 cup CANOLA OIL
1 cup CIDER VINEGAR
1/3 cup SUGAR

4 tsp. SALT
1/2 tsp. PEPPER

2 cans (16 oz. ea.) RED KIDNEY BEANS, drained
2 cans (16 oz. ea.) WHOLE BABY CARROTS, drained

1/2 cup finely chopped ONION
3 pkgs. (10 oz. ea.) FROZEN BROCCOLI SPEARS

Combine marinade ingredients. Place beans and carrots in a 13 x 9 glass casserole dish and sprinkle with onion. Cook broccoli according to package directions; drain well. Layer broccoli over top of bean mixture. Pour marinade over all, cover and refrigerate overnight. When ready to serve, place carrots at one end of serving dish, beans at the other and arrange broccoli in the center.

Zucchini Relish

"This recipe was handed down from my grandmother."

Patricia Henderson—Prince George

4 cups chopped ONION
3 1/2 cups chopped GREEN
   BELL PEPPER
2 1/2 cups grated ZUCCHINI
5 Tbsp. SALT
2 1/2 cups VINEGAR
3/4 tsp. CORNSTARCH

6 cups SUGAR
3/4 tsp. TURMERIC
1 Tbsp. DRY MUSTARD
1/2 tsp. CELERY SEEDS
3/4 tsp. NUTMEG
1/2 tsp. PEPPER

In a large mixing bowl, combine onion, bell peppers, zucchini and salt; let stand overnight and then drain. In a large saucepan, heat remaining ingredients to boiling; add vegetable mixture and cook slowly until vegetables are tender. While hot, pour into sterilized jars and seal.

Green Tomato Catsup

"This was my great-grandmother's recipe. My grandmother also made this each fall, using the last tomatoes of summer. It is an especially delicious addition to baked beans or served with pinto or navy beans."

Teresa Maddox—Amherst

4 qts. sliced GREEN TOMATOES
1/4 cup SALT
1 qt. VINEGAR
6 cups SUGAR
1 GREEN BELL PEPPER, chopped
1 RED BELL PEPPER, chopped
2 lg. ONIONS, chopped
1 head CABBAGE, chopped
3 Tbsp. PICKLING SPICES, wrapped in cheesecloth and tied

Place tomato slices in a large bowl, add enough water to cover and stir in salt; soak slices overnight. The next day, rinse tomato slices well and then drain. Add all ingredients to a large saucepan and simmer until vegetables are tender. Pour into sterilized jars and seal.

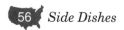

Crab Recipes

Jim Casey from Casey's Seafood in Newport News on Chesapeake Bay provided the recipes in this section. He originally owned a crab plant where the women in the area purchased their crabmeat. Over the years a 'recipe swap' developed. Jim has assembled the best of them for this collection.

Cheezy Crab Hors D'oeuvres

1 pkg. (8 oz.) CREAM CHEESE, softened
1 Tbsp. MILK
1 Tbsp. minced ONION
1/2 tsp. HORSERADISH
1 cup any WHITE CRABMEAT
SALT and PEPPER to taste
1/4 cup slivered ALMONDS

In a medium bowl, blend cream cheese, milk, onion and horseradish. Gently fold in crabmeat. Add salt and pepper. Butter a shallow baking dish, add crabmeat mixture and sprinkle almonds over top. Bake at 350° about 20 minutes or until lightly browned on top. Serve hot with crackers.

Crab Information

Jumbo Lump	Largest white pieces of crabmeat from the body portion adjacent to backfin appendage.
Backfin	A blend of large white lump pieces and special meat.
Special	Flaked white meat from the body portion of the crab.
Claw	This meat has a darker tint, but a sweeter flavor.
Cocktail Claw	Clawmeat intact on the claw, outer shell removed.

Hot Crabmeat Canapés

8 oz. any WHITE CRABMEAT
6 Tbsp. MAYONNAISE
SALT and PEPPER to taste

24 thin CRACKERS
shredded SHARP CHEDDAR
   CHEESE

In a small bowl, combine crabmeat, mayonnaise and salt and pepper, mixing well. Spread each cracker with 1 teaspoon of mixture and place on a baking sheet. Sprinkle with shredded cheddar cheese. Broil until cheese has melted and is lightly browned. Serve immediately.

Crabwiches

8 oz. BUTTER or MARGARINE, softened
1 jar KRAFT® OLD ENGLISH CHEESE SPREAD
1 1/2 tsp. MAYONNAISE
1/4 tsp. GARLIC SALT
SALT and PEPPER to taste
1/2 lb. any WHITE CRABMEAT
2 ENGLISH MUFFINS, split and lightly toasted
PAPRIKA

In a medium bowl, mix all ingredients (except crabmeat, muffins and paprika) until smooth. Add crabmeat. Spread on toasted English muffin halves and sprinkle with paprika. Bake at 350° for 12 minutes or until browned and bubbly.

 **About Crabs**

Any of a large variety of crustaceans (animals with a shell) with 10 legs, the front two have pincers. Along the Atlantic coasts, blue crabs are the major catch. All live crabs should be used on the day they are purchased. Refrigerate them until just before cooking. Cook raw crabmeat within 24 hours after the crab dies. Frozen, canned or pasteurized crabs are also available. Pasteurized crabmeat may be stored, unopened, in the refrigerator (33-38°) for up to 1 year and should be used within 4 days of opening.

Crab Soup

1/2 cup each, finely chopped: CELERY, GREEN ONION and
    GREEN BELL PEPPER
1/2 cup BUTTER or MARGARINE, melted
2 cans (10.75 oz. ea.) CONDENSED POTATO SOUP
1 can (17 oz.) CREAMED CORN
1 1/2 cups HALF AND HALF
1 1/2 cups MILK
2 BAY LEAVES
1 Tbsp. THYME
1/2 tsp. GARLIC POWDER
1/2 tsp. WHITE PEPPER
1 lb. any WHITE CRABMEAT

In a medium skillet sauté celery, green onion and bell
pepper in butter until tender; set aside. Place remaining
ingredients, except crabmeat, in a large saucepan. While
gradually adding vegetables, cook and stir over low heat until
thoroughly heated. Add crabmeat and heat to serving temperature. Remove bay leaves before serving.

Makes 10-12 cups.

Crab Salad

1 lb. any WHITE CRABMEAT, flaked
1 cup chopped CELERY
1/2 cup chopped GREEN BELL PEPPER
4 HARD-BOILED EGGS, chopped
1/4 cup chopped ONION
1 LEMON, juiced
3 Tbsp. INDIA RELISH*
MAYONNAISE

In a large bowl, blend all ingredients, adding mayonnaise
to taste. Refrigerate at least 2 hours before serving. Serve on
beds of **LETTUCE LEAVES.** Garnish with **PARSLEY** and **LEMON
WEDGES.**

Serves 6.

Note: India Relish is made with a combination of cucumbers, tomatoes, bell peppers and a variety of spices. It can be
purchased in grocery stores.

Puffing Crab

2 Tbsp. BUTTER or MARGARINE	1 lb. any WHITE CRABMEAT
2 Tbsp. FLOUR	SALT and PEPPER to taste
1 cup HOT MILK	Dash CAYENNE
3 EGGS, separated	1 Tbsp. PAPRIKA
1/2 cup MAYONNAISE	

In a medium saucepan, melt butter. Slowly stir in flour until blended. Slowly stir in milk. Beat egg yolks with mayonnaise and stir into mixture. Add crabmeat, salt, pepper and cayenne. Cool. In a small bowl, beat egg whites until stiff. Fold into crab mixture. Spoon into a greased 1 1/2-quart casserole dish. Dust with paprika and bake at 400° for 10 minutes or until browned and puffed.

Serves 4.

Crab Newburg

1/2 cup BUTTER or MARGARINE	2 Tbsp. chopped ONION
3 Tbsp. FLOUR	3 EGG YOLKS
2 cups CREAM	2 Tbsp. SHERRY
1/2 tsp. SALT	1 lb. LUMP CRABMEAT
1/2 tsp. PAPRIKA	TOAST or TART SHELLS

In a medium saucepan, melt butter and stir in flour. Gradually stir in cream, salt, paprika and onion. In a small bowl, beat egg yolks with sherry and add to mixture. Cool until thickened and smooth. Stir in crabmeat. Serve on toast or in tart shells.

Serves 6.

Tidewater-Style Crab Cakes

1 lb. any WHITE CRABMEAT	1 tsp. HONEY MUSTARD
8 SALTINE CRACKERS, crushed	1 tsp. MAYONNAISE
1 EGG	OLD BAY SEASONING®

In a large bowl, mix all ingredients. Shape into cakes. Place on a plate and refrigerate for 20 to 30 minutes to set. Fry in hot oil until golden brown.

Makes 4 crab cakes.

Crab-Stuffed Mushrooms

24 lg. MUSHROOMS
1 Tbsp. FLOUR
SALT and PEPPER to taste
1/4 tsp. CELERY SALT
Dash CAYENNE
1/4 cup MARGARINE
1/2 cup LIGHT CREAM

1 lb. any WHITE CRABMEAT
1 Tbsp. chopped PARSLEY
1 Tbsp. SHERRY
2 Tbsp. grated PARMESAN
   CHEESE
PAPRIKA (optional)

Rinse and dry mushrooms then remove and chop stems. Set aside. In a medium saucepan, blend flour and seasonings with margarine. Gradually add cream and cook, stirring constantly, until thick and smooth. Add 2 tablespoons of mushroom stems, parsley and sherry. Stir in crabmeat. Stuff mushroom caps with mixture and place in a greased baking pan. Sprinkle with cheese and paprika. Bake at 350° for 15 to 20 minutes or until tops are lightly browned.

Serves 6.

Chesapeake Bay

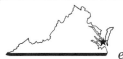

Chesapeake Bay, America's largest estuary, holds 19 trillion gallons of water, with an average depth of 21 feet. Forty-six rivers and streams flow into the bay, providing the perfect environment for Virginia's famed Chesapeake Bay blue crabs.

Virginia Crab Imperial

2 EGGS
1/4 tsp. DRY MUSTARD
Dash WHITE PEPPER
2 lbs. any WHITE CRABMEAT
4 Tbsp. PIMENTO

2 1/4 tsp. + 1/4 cup
   MAYONNAISE
1/2 cup grated PARMESAN
   CHEESE

In a large bowl, beat eggs with mustard and pepper. Add crabmeat, pimento and 2 1/4 teaspoons mayonnaise. Spoon into a 2-quart buttered casserole dish. Spread 1/4 cup mayonnaise over top and sprinkle with Parmesan cheese. Bake in a preheated 350° oven for 30 minutes or until golden and bubbly.

Serves 6.

Crabmeat Au Gratin

1 lb. BACKFIN CRABMEAT	Buttered BREAD CRUMBS
2 cups WHITE SAUCE	PAPRIKA
1/2 tsp. LEMON JUICE	Grated CHEESE
1 1/2 tsp. grated ONION	

In a large bowl, combine crabmeat with **White Sauce**, lemon juice and onion. Turn into a greased casserole dish. Top with buttered bread crumbs, paprika and grated cheese. Bake at 375° for 20 to 25 minutes or until browned.

Serves 4.

White Sauce

4 Tbsp. BUTTER or MARGARINE	SALT and PEPPER to taste
4 Tbsp. FLOUR	2 cups MILK

In a medium saucepan, melt butter over low heat. Add flour, salt and pepper, stirring until well-blended. Remove from heat. Gradually stir in milk and return to heat. Cook, stirring constantly, until thick and smooth.

Spicy Deviled Crabs

1 Tbsp. DRY MUSTARD
1 tsp. SALT
1/2 tsp. CAYENNE
3/4 cup VINEGAR
1 lb. CLAW CRABMEAT, shells reserved
4 oz. BUTTER or MARGARINE, melted
1/2 cup CRACKER CRUMBS
PAPRIKA

In a medium bowl, mix mustard, salt, cayenne and vinegar until well-blended. Add crabmeat. Stir in melted butter. Add cracker crumbs, mixing well. Pack mixture into crab shells or natural baking shells and sprinkle with paprika. Bake at 350° for 20 minutes.

Serves 4 to 6.

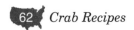

Peanut Recipes

These recipes were provided by the
Virginia-Carolina Peanut Promotion Association

Sweetheart Cookies

1 cup BUTTER, softened
1 1/3 cups GRANULATED SUGAR
1 1/3 cups packed LIGHT BROWN SUGAR
2 EGGS, beaten
1 tsp. VANILLA
1 1/2 cups ALL-PURPOSE FLOUR
1 tsp. BAKING SODA
3 cups QUICK-COOKING ROLLED OATS
1 1/2 cups chopped roasted PEANUTS
1 pkg. (6 oz.) SEMI-SWEET CHOCOLATE CHIPS

Preheat oven to 375°. Cream butter and sugars in a large mixing bowl; add eggs and vanilla. Beat until fluffy. Mix flour with baking soda in large bowl, add oats and toss to coat. Add flour mixture to butter-sugar mixture one cup at a time until completely mixed. Stir in peanuts and chocolate chips. Batter will be stiff. Drop from a teaspoon onto a cookie sheet. Bake for 10-12 minutes.

Makes 6 dozen.

George Washington Carver

In 1860, with the outbreak of the Civil War, Northern soldiers, as well as Southern, used the peanut as a food. In 1903, George Washington Carver began research at Tuskegee Institute that led to many improvements in horticulture and the development of more than 300 uses for peanuts (including shoe polish and shaving cream). He proposed that peanuts be planted as a rotation crop in the Southeast cotton-growing areas. For his work in promoting its cultivation and consumption, Carver is considered the father of the peanut industry.

Peanut Soup

1 med. ONION, chopped
2 stalks CELERY, chopped
3 Tbsp. BUTTER
3 Tbsp. ALL-PURPOSE FLOUR
4 cups CHICKEN BROTH
1 cup CREAMY PEANUT BUTTER
1 cup LIGHT CREAM or HALF AND HALF
1 Tbsp. LEMON JUICE
4 Tbsp. chopped roasted PEANUTS

In a large saucepan, sauté onion and celery in butter until tender, about 10 minutes. Add flour and stir until well-blended. Stir in chicken broth and simmer for 30 minutes. Remove from heat and let cool for 15 minutes. Pureé in food processor. Return to saucepan and add peanut butter, cream and lemon juice. Let simmer, stirring occasionally, for 5 minutes. Do not boil. Garnish each serving with chopped peanuts.

Serves 6.

Food Value of the Peanut

Raw peanut with skins: 47.5% fat, 26.0% protein, 18.6% carbohydrates, 5.6% water and 2.3% other.

Peanut Butter Muffins

2 cups ALL-PURPOSE FLOUR
1 Tbsp. BAKING POWDER
1 cup MILK
2 EGGS

1/2 cup SUGAR
1/2 cup CREAMY PEANUT
   BUTTER
1 tsp. SALT

Preheat oven to 400°. In a bowl, combine flour and baking powder and set aside. Place milk, eggs, sugar, peanut butter and salt in a blender container, cover and blend. Pour over dry ingredients and stir just to moisten. Fill greased muffin pans 2/3 full. Bake in a 400° oven 15 to 20 minutes.

Makes 12 muffins.

Chicken-Peanut Salad Croissants

2 cups cooked, cubed CHICKEN
1/2 cup coarsely chopped
    PEANUTS
1/4 cup chopped GREEN ONIONS
1/4 cup chopped CELERY

MAYONNAISE
BLACK PEPPER
4 CROISSANTS
ROMAINE or RED LEAF
    LETTUCE

In a large bowl, mix chicken with peanuts. Stir in onions and celery. Add mayonnaise to moisten and pepper to taste. Spread on bottom halves of croissants. Top with lettuce and add croissant top.

Makes 4 sandwiches.

> *Peanuts are native to South America where Indians were growing them at least 1,000 years ago.*

Pumpkin & Peanut Bread

4 EGGS
3 cups SUGAR
1 cup PEANUT OIL
1/3 cup WATER
1 can (30 oz.) PUMPKIN PIE FILLING
3 1/2 cups ALL-PURPOSE FLOUR
2 tsp. BAKING SODA
1 1/2 tsp. SALT
1 tsp. CINNAMON
1 1/2 cups chopped DATES
1 cup chopped roasted PEANUTS

Preheat oven to 350°. Grease and flour three (5 x 9) loaf pans. In large bowl, beat eggs slightly. Gradually stir in sugar, oil, water and pumpkin pie filling. Add flour, soda, salt and cinnamon and mix well. Stir in dates and peanuts. Pour 1/3 of the batter into each loaf pan. Bake for 1 hour or until bread pulls away from sides. Cool in pans on wire rack for 10 minutes, then remove from pans and finish cooling loaves on rack.

Makes 3 loaves.

Broccoli Nut Casserole

2 pkgs. (10 oz. ea.) frozen chopped BROCCOLI
1/2 tsp. SALT
1 can (10.75 oz.) CREAM OF MUSHROOM SOUP
1 cup MAYONNAISE
3/4 cup chopped roasted PEANUTS
2 EGGS, well-beaten
1 med. ONION, chopped (or 1 1/2 tsp. dried onion flakes)
1/4 cup BUTTER, melted
1 cup grated SHARP CHEDDAR CHEESE
2 cups dry BREAD CRUMBS

Cook broccoli with salt according to package directions; drain and place in a mixing bowl. Add soup, mayonnaise and peanuts. Mix well. Add eggs and onion, mixing well. In another bowl, pour melted butter over bread crumbs. Pour broccoli mixture into a greased 2-quart casserole dish. Sprinkle with grated cheese and top with buttered bread crumbs. Bake at 350° for 30 minutes.

Serves 6 to 8.

About Peanuts

The peanut is a fruit of the peanut plant and a legume, not a nut. Peanuts bear seeds in containers called pods (shells), usually two in each. The peanut plant is unusual because its pods develop underground. For this reason, peanuts are

often called groundnuts. *Other names for peanuts include* goobers, goober peas, groundpeas *and* pindas.

Peanut flowers open at dawn, wither and then fall from the plant. The base of each fertilized flower then begins to grow, forming a peg (a stalklike stem). The peg pushes down into the ground, swells and grows into a peanut pod.

Heavenly Peanut Torte

3 cups finely chopped
   roasted PEANUTS
2 Tbsp. ALL-PURPOSE FLOUR
2 tsp. BAKING POWDER
6 EGGS, separated
1 1/2 cups SUGAR
1 1/2 tsp. VANILLA EXTRACT

1/4 tsp. SALT
1/2 cup POWDERED SUGAR
1 pint WHIPPING CREAM
1/2 cup grated SWEET
   CHOCOLATE
PEANUT halves, for garnish

Line the bottom of three (9-inch) round cake pans with greased waxed paper; set aside. In a large bowl, mix together peanuts, flour and baking powder. In another bowl, combine egg yolks and 1 cup sugar; beat until thick and light in color. Add vanilla, then stir into peanut mixture. In a medium bowl, combine egg whites and salt and beat until stiff, but not dry. Gradually add remaining 1/2 cup sugar, beating until stiff peaks form. Gently fold egg whites into peanut mixture. Pour into prepared pans. Bake at 325° for 30 minutes. Allow to cool for about 15 minutes and then loosen cake layers around edges and turn out of pans onto wire racks. Remove waxed paper. Wrap cooled cakes and store at room temperature. Combine powdered sugar and whipping cream, beat until soft peaks form. Chill. When ready to serve, spread whipped cream mixture on each cake layer, sprinkle with grated chocolate and stack. Garnish top with peanut halves.

Serves 12-16.

About 2.4 billion pounds of peanuts are consumed in the U.S. each year, 50% of them are used in peanut butter.

Peanut Stuffing

Use as a stuffing for pork, chicken or turkey.

2 cups dry BREAD CRUMBS
1/4 cup finely chopped ONION
1/2 cup chopped CELERY
1/2 cup chopped roasted PEANUTS

1/8 tsp. BLACK PEPPER
2 Tbsp. BUTTER, melted
1/4 to 1/2 cup WATER or
   BROTH

In a large bowl, combine all ingredients except water. Add enough water to moisten.

Peanut Butter-Bacon Rollups

1/4 cup CRUNCHY PEANUT BUTTER
2 Tbsp. BUTTER, melted
1/2 cup WATER
2 cups PACKAGED HERB-SEASONED STUFFING MIX
1 EGG, slightly beaten
1/2 lb. BULK PORK SAUSAGE
1/4 cup chopped roasted PEANUTS
3/4 lb. sliced BACON

In a large bowl, mix peanut butter, butter, water and stuffing mix. Stir in egg, sausage and peanuts; blend well. Chill for about 1 hour. Shape into small balls or oblongs. Cut bacon slices into thirds. Wrap each piece of stuffing mixture with a piece of bacon and fasten with a toothpick. Place on a rack in a shallow pan. Bake in a preheated 375° oven 30 to 35 minutes. Turn halfway through cooking. Drain on paper towels and serve hot. Stack on serving plate and garnish with **CHERRY TOMATOES** and **PARSLEY**

Note: Rollups may be made ahead of time and frozen before baking. To serve, thaw and bake as directed above.

Makes about 4 dozen.

Buckeyes

1 cup BUTTER, softened
1 pkg. (16 oz.) POWDERED SUGAR
1 jar (12 oz.) CRUNCHY PEANUT BUTTER
1 pkg. (12 oz.) SEMI-SWEET CHOCOLATE CHIPS

Combine butter, sugar and peanut butter in a medium bowl and blend until smooth. Roll into 1-inch balls. Chill. Melt chocolate chips in the top of a double boiler over hot (not boiling) water or in microwave (follow package directions). Dip balls in chocolate mixture one at a time. Allow to cool on waxed paper.

Makes about 5 dozen.

Breads

Apple Butter-Pecan Muffins

Using apple butter in this recipe eliminates the need for any additional spices and produces a very moist muffin.

Developed for Ann's Apple Butter by Janice Therese Mancuso

1 lg. APPLE, peeled, thinly sliced and chopped
1/2 tsp. CINNAMON
1 Tbsp. plus 1/2 cup SUGAR
1 stick BUTTER or MARGARINE, softened
1 cup ANN'S® APPLE BUTTER
2 EGGS
2 cups FLOUR
1 Tbsp. BAKING POWDER
1 cup coarsely chopped PECANS
BROWN SUGAR

Preheat oven to 375°. In a medium bowl, toss chopped apples with cinnamon and 1 tablespoon sugar to coat thoroughly. Set aside. In a mixing bowl, cream butter, apple butter and 1/2 cup sugar until well blended. Add eggs, mix well. Add flour and baking powder, blending well. Stir in chopped apples and pecans. Spoon into greased or paper-lined muffin tins. Sprinkle with brown sugar. Bake 15 to 20 minutes.

Makes 18 muffins.

Jamming Muffins

*Rowena's® Carrot Jam has often been described as
"a carrot cake in a jar."*

Rowena's, Inc.—Norfolk

1 3/4 cups FLOUR	2 EGGS
1/2 cup SUGAR	2/3 cup MILK
1 Tbsp. BAKING POWDER	1/3 cup BUTTER, melted
1/4 tsp. SALT	ROWENA'S® CARROT JAM

In a large mixing bowl, combine first four ingredients. In another mixing bowl, lightly beat eggs; add milk and butter and stir. Pour egg mixture into dry ingredients and stir until moistened. Spoon half of the batter into 12 greased muffin cups. Add a generous teaspoon of carrot jam to the center of each muffin. Spoon the remaining batter over jam. Bake at 400° for 20-25 minutes.

Makes 12 muffins.

Ham & Cheese Bread

Lucille Barrett—S. Wallace Edwards & Sons, Inc., Surry

2 cups ALL-PURPOSE FLOUR
1/2 tsp. BAKING POWDER
1/2 tsp. BAKING SODA
1 cup shredded MEDIUM or SHARP CHEDDAR CHEESE
1 cup BUTTERMILK (can substitute with 1 cup MILK mixed with
    1 Tbsp. VINEGAR)
1/3 cup MARGARINE, melted
2 EGGS
1 cup EDWARDS'® GROUND HAM

In a large bowl combine first four ingredients, blending well. In a medium bowl, mix buttermilk, margarine and eggs. Add to flour mixture. Stir in ham. Grease bottom of a loaf pan. Pour batter into pan and bake at 350° for 45 minutes or until toothpick inserted in center comes out clean.

Chive & Cheddar Cheese Biscuits

Shenandoah Growers Inc.—Harrisonburg

2 cups BISCUIT MIX
3/4 cup shredded CHEDDAR CHEESE
1/4 cup chopped SHENANDOAH GROWERS® fresh CHIVES
1/2 to 1 cup MILK

In a large bowl, blend biscuit mix, cheese and chives. Mix gently with 1/2 cup milk, adding additional milk as needed to form a soft ball. Turn onto floured board and knead gently 6 to 8 times. Roll dough out to 3/4-inch thickness and cut with biscuit cutter. Place biscuits on a lightly greased baking sheet and brush tops with milk. Bake at 450° for 10 minutes or until golden brown.

Fredericksburg & Spotsylvania National Military Park

The 8,400 acres of this park which lie in and around Fredericksburg, include four great battlefields of the Civil War: Fredericksburg, Chancellorsville, The Wilderness and Spotsylvania Court House.

Virginia Ham Biscuits

Vonnie Beaver Edwards—S. Wallace Edwards & Sons, Inc., Surry

2 cups FLOUR
4 tsp. BAKING POWDER
1/2 cup EDWARDS'® VIRGINIA
    GROUND HAM

2 Tbsp. SHORTENING
3/4 cup MILK

In a mixing bowl, sift flour and baking powder together. Mix in ham. Cut in shortening with pastry blender until mixture has the consistency of meal. Add milk, handling as little as possible. Pat dough out with hands or roll out on a sheet of waxed paper dusted with flour. Cut out biscuits and bake in a 425° oven until browned.

Spoon Bread

"In 1979 my mother entered a cook-off using cornmeal that was ground by the Flowerdew Hundred wind-powered gristmill. She won first place with this great recipe!"

Dale P. Dailey—Hopewell

2 cups CORNMEAL	3 Tbsp. BUTTER
1 Tbsp. SUGAR	1 cup BUTTERMILK
1 1/2 tsp. SALT	2 EGGS, separated
2 cups BOILING WATER	1/2 tsp. BAKING SODA

In a large mixing bowl, combine cornmeal, sugar and salt; mix well. Add water, butter and buttermilk; stir. Beat egg yolks and baking soda together; add to mixture. Beat egg whites until stiff; fold into mixture. Pour into greased baking pan. Bake at 350° for 45-50 minutes.

Grandma's Whole-Wheat Rolls

"This was my grandmother's recipe. These rolls were always a favorite for family gatherings."

Linda Barrett Roark—Abingdon

1 cup WARM WATER	1/2 cup HOT WATER
2 Tbsp. SUGAR	2 tsp. SALT
2 pkgs. active dry YEAST	2 EGGS, beaten
1/2 cup SHORTENING	3 cups WHOLE-WHEAT FLOUR
1/2 cup SUGAR	2-3 cups ALL-PURPOSE FLOUR
1/2 cup MILK	

In a small bowl, combine warm water and 2 tablespoons sugar; add yeast and set aside. In a large mixing bowl, combine shortening, sugar, milk, hot water and salt. Stir until shortening melts; let cool. When cool, combine mixtures, adding eggs and whole-wheat flour. Beat well. Add 2-3 cups all-purpose flour to make a soft dough and knead for 5 minutes, keeping dough as soft as possible. Place in a greased bowl and refrigerate until ready to use, or form into rolls immediately. Place in greased pans; let rise 1-2 hours. Bake at 400° for 20 minutes or until brown.

Grandma's Cornbread

"Grandma's cornbread was simple and good. In later years I added a few ingredients to spice it up at our hunting camps."

Harold Witt II—Roanoke

2 EGGS, beaten
2 Tbsp. OIL
1 3/4 cups BUTTERMILK

2 cups CORNMEAL
2 Tbsp. finely chopped ONION
2 Tbsp. HOT SAUCE

Preheat oven to 350°. Heat a greased cast-iron skillet in the oven. In a medium mixing bowl, combine all ingredients and mix well. Pour into a hot skillet and bake at 350° for 30 minutes or until bread pulls away from the sides.

Southern Cornbread

"This version of Southern cornbread has been around for over one hundred years. In the early days they raised their own corn and ground their own flour. We still grind our own corn, but our flour is store-bought."

Tenecia Ann Hackney—Birchleaf

3 1/2 Tbsp. VEGETABLE OIL
1 cup ALL-PURPOSE FLOUR
2 tsp. BAKING POWDER
1/4 tsp. of BAKING SODA
1 1/2 tsp. SALT
2 cups homeground WHITE or
    YELLOW CORNMEAL
2 cups BUTTERMILK

Preheat oven to 400°. Grease an 8-inch cast-iron skillet with vegetable oil and heat it in the oven for 5-6 minutes as you stir together the cornbread dough. Combine all ingredients in a large mixing bowl; mix well (batter will be very thick). Pour into heated skillet. Bake at 400° for 35-40 minutes or until golden brown. Let "pone" cool slightly before cutting.

If using self-raising cornmeal and self-rising flour omit baking powder, baking soda and salt and decrease flour to 1/2 cup.

Shelby's Cornbread

"I am a coal miner's daughter, born in Kentucky and raised in Virginia. My children did not like the taste of plain cornbread so I devised a way to make it more tasty and have been using this recipe ever since. It's always requested for family get-togethers."

Shelby J. (Adkins) Barton—Haysi

1 Tbsp. WESSON® OIL or LARD
2 cups SELF-RISING CORNMEAL
1/4 cup SELF-RISING FLOUR
1/3 tsp. SALT
1 EGG, beaten
1 cup BUTTERMILK
6 strips BACON,
   cooked and crumbled
COLD WATER

Preheat oven to 350°. Grease a large cast-iron skillet, add oil and heat in oven. When pan is hot, drain oil into a medium mixing bowl. Add remaining ingredients to bowl (adding cold water as needed to mix well). Pour into heated skillet. Bake at 350° for 30-35 minutes or until golden brown. Serve hot or cold.

Aunt Liza's
Rhubarb Marmalade

"This is my grandmother's recipe. It is wonderful and absolutely delicious on homemade biscuits."

Joann M. Vicars—Bristol Virginia Police Department, Bristol

1 LEMON
2 ORANGES
4 lbs. RHUBARB, chopped
1 lb. SEEDLESS RAISINS
3 lbs. SUGAR

Squeeze juice from lemon and oranges and combine with rhubarb in a large pot. Chop lemon rind, orange rinds and raisins; add to rhubarb mixture and mix well. Let stand for 30 minutes. Add sugar, bring to a boil, then reduce heat to simmering and cook for 1 hour, stirring frequently. When mixture thickens, pour into sterilized jars, glasses or crock; seal when cool.

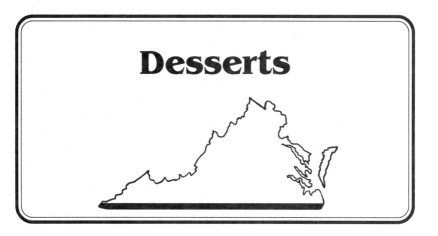

Desserts

Ola's Fruitcake Cookies

"My mother's friend, Ola, made these for us each Christmas.
This is her grandmother's recipe."

Virginia Miller—Charlottesville

3 cups RAISINS
1/2 cup BOURBON
1/4 cup BUTTER, softened
1/2 cup packed BROWN
    SUGAR
2 EGGS
1 1/2 cups FLOUR
1 1/2 tsp. BAKING SODA

1 1/2 tsp. CINNAMON
1/2 tsp. NUTMEG
1/2 tsp. ground CLOVES
1 lb. halved PECANS
1 lb. CANDIED or MARASCHINO
    CHERRIES, cut in half
1/2 lb. CANDIED CITRON, diced

Place raisins in a bowl and add bourbon. Mix well and let stand for 1 hour. In a large mixing bowl, cream together butter and brown sugar; add eggs and mix well. In another bowl, combine flour, baking soda and spices; mix well. Gradually add the flour mixture to the creamed ingredients, beating until smooth after each addition. Stir in raisin mixture, pecans, cherries and citron. Drop by teaspoonfuls onto a greased cookie sheet. Bake at 325° for 15 minutes or until firm. Cool on a wire rack. Store in airtight container.

Yields 7-8 dozen.

Peanut Brittle

Ivea J. Logan—Elberon

2 cups RAW PEANUTS
1 1/2 cups SUGAR
3/4 cup DARK CORN SYRUP
2 tsp. BAKING SODA

In a heavy saucepan, stir peanuts, sugar and corn syrup together. Cook over medium heat, stirring often, about 20 minutes or to hard crack stage on a candy thermometer. Lightly grease a baking sheet with margarine. Have baking soda measured in small bowl. When peanut brittle has reached hard crack, remove from heat and briskly stir in baking soda. Pour evenly over baking sheet; do not spread. Let cool. When cool, brittle will pop out of baking sheet in one piece. Break into pieces and store in an airtight container.

Mom's Old-Fashioned Gingerbread

"My dad was a coal miner with thirteen children. To economize, we made our own molasses and used it in place of white sugar. All of us looked forward to Saturday and Mom's Gingerbread."

Betty Lou Collius—Clinchco

1/2 cup WHITE SUGAR
1 1/2 cups packed BROWN SUGAR
3/4 cup MARGARINE, softened
3 EGGS
1/2 cup BUTTERMILK
1/2 cup MOLASSES

1 Tbsp. VANILLA
6-8 cups SELF-RISING FLOUR
1/2 tsp. BAKING SODA
3-4 Tbsp. ground GINGER

In a large mixing bowl, cream sugars, margarine and eggs together; add buttermilk, molasses and vanilla. In a separate bowl, sift flour, baking soda and ginger together; add to creamed mixture and stir well. Add enough additional flour to form a soft dough. Shape dough into small balls and pat out on a greased cookie sheet. Bake at 350° for 10-15 minutes or until done.

Orange Candy Squares

*"My mother-in-law always made this bread as
a special treat at Christmas."*

Virginia L. Thompson—Abingdon

4 EGGS
2 1/4 cups packed
    BROWN SUGAR
3 cups FLOUR

1 cup chopped PECANS
1/4 cup CANDIED ORANGE
    SLICES
1/2 cup WHITE SUGAR

In a large mixing bowl, combine eggs, brown sugar and flour
and mix well. Cut up orange slices and dredge in flour. Add
orange slices and pecans to batter, then pour into a greased flat
cake pan. Bake at 350° for 45 minutes. Cool, cut into squares
and roll in white sugar to coat. Store in a covered container.

Arlington National Cemetery

*Across the Potomac River from Washing-
ton D.C., is one of the largest and most
famous national cemeteries in the U. S. William H. Taft
and John F. Kennedy are the only Presidents to be buried
here. An eternal flame marks the grave of President Kennedy.*

Ancestral Pound Cake

*"This recipe is from the late 1800s. It was handed down from my
grandmother to my mother, to me and now I have given it to my
children. This cake is enjoyed when sliced, slightly toasted and
topped with a scoop of vanilla ice cream."*

Lion Bill Hadden—Lynchburg

2 sticks BUTTER
2 cups SUGAR
5 lg. EGGS

2 1/2 cups sifted FLOUR
3/4 tsp. VANILLA
2 Tbsp. HOT WATER

In a large mixing bowl, cream together butter and sugar
until light and fluffy. Add eggs one at a time, beating well after
each addition. Fold in flour; add vanilla and hot water. Bake
in a greased and floured tube pan at 325° for 60-65 minutes or
until toothpick inserted in center comes out clean. Cool in pan
for 10 minutes; turn out onto cooling rack.

Peach Ice Cream

"My aunt 'Jenny' (Annie Virginia Good Heinzmann) gave me her recipe for this unusual ice cream. It was published in Southern Living Magazine years ago."

Betty Weatherholtz Fitzgerald—Bedford

1 1/4 cups SUGAR
1 1/2 Tbsp. CORNSTARCH
1/4 tsp. SALT
3 EGGS, beaten
1 1/2 Tbsp. ALL-PURPOSE
   FLOUR
2 cups MILK
2 cups sliced fresh PEACHES

1/3 cup SUGAR
1 pkg. (3 oz.) PEACH GELATIN
3/4 cup BOILING WATER
3 pts. frozen non-dairy COFFEE
   CREAMER, thawed
1/4 cup SUGAR
1/2 cup SOUR CREAM

In a large saucepan, combine first five ingredients. Mix well and then stir in milk. Cook mixture over medium heat, stirring constantly until smooth and thickened. Remove from heat and chill for 2-3 hours. Place peaches in a saucepan and cook over medium heat until bubbly, stirring constantly. Stir in 1/3 cup sugar. Place peach mixture in blender and blend until smooth; set aside. Dissolve gelatin in boiling water and allow to cool. Combine coffee creamer and 1/4 cup sugar in a large bowl and stir well. Gradually stir in egg mixture. Add puréed peaches, gelatin mixture and sour cream. Beat mixture with a wire whisk until smooth. Pour into freezer container of a 1-gallon freezer and freeze according to manufacturer's instructions. Let sit for 2 hours before serving.

Daddy's Burnt Caramel Platter Candy

Debbie Greene Mullins—Clinchco

• 3 cups SUGAR   • 1 pt. MILK   • 1/4 lb. BUTTER

Brown sugar in a cast-iron skillet. Add milk and boil 20-30 minutes or until thick. Remove from heat, add butter and stir thoroughly. Pour onto a buttered platter and when set, break into pieces.

Ol' Virginia Fresh Apple Cake

Caroline S. Taylor—Charlottesville

3 EGGS
1 1/2 cups WESSON® OIL
2 cups SUGAR
3 cups FLOUR
1 tsp. BAKING SODA
1 tsp. SALT

1 tsp. CINNAMON
2 tsp. VANILLA
3 cups finely chopped APPLES
1 cup chopped NUTS
1 cup flaked COCONUT

In a large bowl, beat together eggs, oil and sugar. In another bowl, sift together flour, baking soda, salt and cinnamon. Add flour mixture to creamed ingredients and mix well. Add vanilla and fold in apples, nuts and coconut. Pour batter into a large greased and floured tube pan. Bake at 350° for 45-60 minutes.

Grandma's Butterscotch Pie

"This recipe was passed down to my mother from my grand-mother. My mother gave it to me, and I am now passing it on to my daughters and granddaughters!"

Kyma Simmons—Goodview

5 Tbsp. FLOUR
1 cup packed BROWN SUGAR
3 Tbsp. BUTTER
1 1/2 cups MILK

2 EGGS, separated
1 tsp. VANILLA
1 (9-inch) baked PIE SHELL

In a saucepan, mix flour, brown sugar and butter; add milk and stir. Cook over medium heat until thick. In a bowl, beat egg yolks, then add 2 tablespoonfuls of brown sugar mixture and mix well. Add yolk mixture into saucepan and continue cooking until mixture again thickens. Stir in vanilla. Pour into pie shell. Beat egg whites until stiff peaks form then layer over pie. Bake at 325° for 10-15 minutes or until top is light brown.

Mother's Hermit Cake

"This is an 'Old Virginia' recipe that my mother used for years and passed on to me. It's been a favorite for 75-100 years!"

Dora G. Evans—Lynchburg

5 cups sifted FLOUR
2 lbs. chopped DATES
1 cup shelled PECANS
   or WALNUTS
2 1/4 cups packed LIGHT
   BROWN SUGAR
3 sticks BUTTER or
   MARGARINE, softened
6 EGGS, beaten

1 tsp. VANILLA
Juice of 1 LEMON
2 tsp. BAKING POWDER
1/4 tsp. SALT
1 tsp. CINNAMON
1/4 tsp. NUTMEG
RED and GREEN CANDIED
   CHERRIES, halved

Flour dates and nuts with 1 cup of the flour. In a large mixing bowl, cream together sugar and butter. Gradually add eggs, mixing well. Stir in vanilla and lemon juice. Add baking powder, salt, cinnamon and nutmeg to creamed mixture and mix well. Fold in dates and nuts. Pour batter into a greased and floured cake pan. Bake at 250° for 3 hours or until toothpick inserted in center comes out clean. Cool in pan for 20 minutes then turn out onto a wire rack and cool completely. Decorate with candied cherries. When cake is cool, wrap it in a soft cloth and sprinkle with **GRAPE JUICE** or **WINE**. Store in a cake tin.

Strawberry-Rhubarb Cobbler

"Our whole family uses this recipe with whatever fruit is in season at the time. Most of our fruit is homegrown."

Debbie Greene Mullins—Clinchco

1 stick BUTTER, softened
1 cup FLOUR
1 cup SUGAR
1 cup MILK

1 1/2 cups halved
   STRAWBERRIES
1 1/2 cups cooked
   RHUBARB

Cut up butter and drop pieces into 9 x 13 pan. In a mixing bowl, combine flour, sugar and milk; mix well. Pour batter into pan; add fruit on top. Bake at 350° for 1 hour.

Grandma Busch's Lemon Meringue Pie

"My grandmother is a wonderful cook. I have many fine memories of family gatherings at her home. She always has this pie made for me when I visit because she knows it is my favorite. She is now 84 years old and still bakes and cooks."

Beverly Busch Hunter—Bedford

1 cup SUGAR	2 Tbsp. MILK
1 1/2 cups WATER	6 Tbsp. LEMON JUICE
1 Tbsp. BUTTER	1 tsp. LEMON RIND
1/4 cup CORNSTARCH	1 (9-inch) baked PIE SHELL
3 Tbsp. WATER	3 EGG WHITES
3 EGGS, separated	6 Tbsp. SUGAR

Preheat oven to 400°. In a double-boiler, combine sugar, water and butter and heat just enough to dissolve the sugar and melt the butter. Combine cornstarch and 3 tablespoons water, add to sugar mixture and cook for 8 minutes or until thickened. In a small bowl, beat egg yolks with milk; stir in a small amount of hot mixture and then add back into the double-boiler and cook for 2 minutes. Remove from heat, add lemon juice and rind and cool slightly. Pour into pie shell. In a bowl, beat egg whites until frothy. Gradually add sugar and beat until stiff but not dry. Pile meringue lightly on top of pie, covering completely. Bake at 400° for 5 minutes or until lightly browned.

Hampton Roads Area

In nautical terms, a "road" is a protected area near shore where ships can safely anchor. Named after the third Earl of Southampton, Hampton Roads is the area where the James, Elizabeth and Nansemond rivers empty into the Chesapeake Bay. The area now includes Norfolk, Virginia Beach, Newport News, Hampton, Portsmouth and other surrounding towns.

Autumn Apple Cheesecake

"You can use any of Virginia's fine apples in this recipe. This cheesecake is delicious all year long, not just in the fall!"

Mary Moyer—Waynesboro

1 cup GRAHAM CRACKER CRUMBS	2 EGGS
3 Tbsp. SUGAR	1/2 tsp. VANILLA
1/2 tsp. CINNAMON	1/3 cup SUGAR
1/4 cup MARGARINE, melted	1/2 tsp. CINNAMON
2 pkgs. (8 oz. ea.) CREAM	4 cups thinly sliced
CHEESE, softened	peeled APPLES
1/2 cup SUGAR	1/4 cup chopped PECANS

In a small bowl, combine crumbs, sugar, cinnamon and margarine; mix well. Press into the bottom of a 9" springform pan. Bake at 350° for 10 minutes. In a bowl, combine cream cheese and sugar; mix until well-blended. Add eggs, one at a time, mixing well after each addition. Blend in vanilla. Pour mixture over crust. Combine sugar and cinnamon in a large bowl and toss apple slices in mixture until well-coated. Spoon apples over cream cheese layer and sprinkle top with nuts. Bake at 350° for 70 minutes. Cool cake before removing rim of pan. Chill.

Old-Fashioned Peanut Butter Fudge

"This fudge has been a family favorite since the early 1960s."

Margie Marie Edwards—Birchleaf

3 cups SUGAR	1 tsp. VANILLA
1 1/2 cups MILK	1 stick BUTTER, softened
Pinch of SALT	2 cups PEANUT BUTTER

In a medium saucepan, mix sugar, milk and salt and cook to soft ball stage. Remove from heat and add vanilla, 3/4 stick of butter and peanut butter. Beat well. Use the remaining butter to grease the bottom of a square baking pan. Pour candy mixture into pan. Let cool and then cut into squares.

Chocolate Buttermilk Cake

"My friend, Janice Abbott, gave me this recipe. She makes this cake for her mother on special occasions."

Dorothy T. Hunter—Bedford

1 cup WATER	1 tsp. BAKING SODA
1 cup SALAD OIL	1 tsp. SALT
1 stick BUTTER	1 tsp. VANILLA
4 Tbsp. COCOA	1/2 cup BUTTERMILK
2 cups FLOUR	2 EGGS
2 cups SUGAR	

In a small saucepan, combine water, oil, butter and cocoa; stir and heat to boiling then set aside to cool. In a large mixing bowl, combine remaining ingredients and mix well. Add cocoa mixture to batter and blend. Pour batter into a greased and floured 9 x 13 pan. Bake at 350° for 35 minutes. Pour ***Chocolate Frosting*** over cake as soon as it is removed from the oven.

Chocolate Frosting

1/2 cup EVAPORATED MILK	1 box (16 oz.) POWDERED
1 stick BUTTER	SUGAR
4 Tbsp. COCOA	1 cup chopped WALNUTS
1 tsp. VANILLA	or PECANS

In a saucepan, combine evaporated milk, butter, cocoa and vanilla; stir and bring to a boil. Blend in powdered sugar and nuts.

Lynchburg

This city served as a supply base for the Confederate Army, and in 1864 the Battle of Lynchburg was fought for those stores. *Known as the "City of Seven Hills", Lynchburg has several 19th- and early 20th-century residential districts, five of which are National Register Historic Districts, including Court House Hill, Diamond Hill, Garland Hill, Federal Hill and Daniel's Hill.*

Cashew Lace Cookies

"A melt-in-your-mouth, crunchy-thin, caramelized brown sugar cookie crunched with cashew bits and drizzled with white chocolate."

Deborah Marshall—Delisheries Ltd., Cape Charles

1 box DELISHERIES® CARAVAN COOKIE MIX
3/4 stick BUTTER, melted
1/4 cup CREAM or HALF AND HALF
1/2 cup packed DARK BROWN SUGAR
1 cup WHITE CHOCOLATE CHIPS

Preheat oven to 350°. Finely chop cashew nuts from cookie mix. Blend mix with butter, cream and sugar. Stir in chopped cashews. Drop by scant teaspoonfuls 2 inches apart on greased cookie sheets. Bake 5 minutes. Remove from oven, cool about 2 minutes then remove quickly from cookie sheet. Allow cookies to cool completely. Melt white chocolate chips. With tines of a fork, drizzle chocolate lightly across cookies. Let set for 1 hour before serving or storing.

Makes 9 dozen.

Fresh Apple Cake

"My father had a large fruit orchard on his farm in Virginia in the early 1900s and grew many varieties of apples. This is one of many of his recipes that have been passed down in our family."

Alma H. Davis—Clintwood

1 1/2 cups WESSON® OIL
2 cups SUGAR
3 EGGS
2 Tbsp. VANILLA
3 cups FLOUR
1 tsp. BAKING SODA
2 Tbsp. CINNAMON
1 tsp. SALT
3 cups peeled, chopped APPLES
1 cup chopped WALNUTS

In a large mixing bowl, cream together oil, sugar and eggs. Add vanilla. In a separate bowl, combine flour, baking soda, cinnamon and salt; mix well. Stir flour mixture into creamed mixture and blend. Fold in apples and walnuts. Pour into a Bundt pan. Bake at 350° for 40-60 minutes or until tests done.

Old-Fashioned Stack Cake

"This recipe was my grandmother's. We had a large family and lived in the coal fields of Virginia."

Ginger Howell—Goodview

3 cups FLOUR	2 EGGS, beaten
1 cup SUGAR	1/2 stick BUTTER, softened
2 Tbsp. BAKING SODA	1 cup MOLASSES
1/2 tsp. GINGER	1 cup BOILING WATER
1/2 tsp. ALLSPICE	Sweetened APPLESAUCE

In a large mixing bowl, combine flour, sugar, baking soda, ginger and allspice. Add eggs, butter, molasses and water and stir until stiff dough forms. Flour hands and divide dough equally into 6 round cake pans, patting into a thin layer. Bake at 350° for 10-12 minutes. When cool, spread sweetened applesauce between layers and stack. Wrap with plastic wrap and refrigerate for at least a day for better flavor.

Did You Know?

The Barter Theatre in Abingdon, founded in 1933, exchanged performance tickets for food in its early years. The Barter is designated "The State Theatre of Virginia."

Theatre Cake

"After attending a performance at Abingdon's Barter Theatre, this cake and a cup of tea or coffee provide a perfect finale!"

Gloria Corcoran—Abingdon

1 cup BUTTER	2 cups ALL-PURPOSE
1 cup SUGAR	FLOUR, sifted
2 fresh LEMON RINDS, grated	1/4 tsp. SALT
5 EGGS	

Preheat oven at 300°. Cream butter, sugar and grated rinds until very light and fluffy, then beat to a very light cream. Add eggs one at a time, beating well after each addition. Sift flour again with salt and fold into butter mixture. Butter and flour a loaf pan, add batter and sprinkle top with additional sugar. Bake for 60-75 minutes.

Old Virginia Pound Cake

"This pound cake, handed down from my great-grandmother, is one of our favorites. Grandma used to serve it with fresh strawberries and whipped cream on top."

Barbara B. Pillow—Phenix

1 lb. BUTTER, softened
3 cups SUGAR
10 lg. EGGS

1 Tbsp. VANILLA
4 cups ALL-PURPOSE
FLOUR

In a large mixing bowl, cream together butter and sugar. Add eggs, one at a time, beating well after each addition. Blend in vanilla. Stir in flour and beat until light and fluffy. Pour batter into a buttered and floured 10-inch tube cake pan. Bake at 300° for 1 1/2 hours.

My Mother-In-Law's Cantaloupe Cream Pie

"This recipe is best when using cantaloupe straight from the garden. Use a fully ripe, sweet smelling cantaloupe for the best tasting pie. It has a lovely peach color, too!"

Carol S. Slater—Sandston

1 cup SUGAR
2 Tbsp. ALL-PURPOSE FLOUR
3 EGGS, beaten
1 cup puréed CANTALOUPE
1 tsp. VANILLA
2 Tbsp. MARGARINE
1 (8-inch) baked PIE SHELL
1 cup WHIPPED CREAM

In a medium saucepan, combine sugar and flour; add eggs and mix well. Stir in cantaloupe and cook mixture over medium heat for 8-10 minutes, stirring until mixture boils and thickens. Stir in vanilla and margarine and then cool. Pour filling into pie shell and spread whipped cream over top. Chill thoroughly.

Plain Cake

"This is an old family recipe."

Deanie A. Whelan—Wicomico Church

1 stick BUTTER	3 EGGS
1 cup MILK	2 cups SUGAR
2 cups FLOUR	1 1/2 Tbsp. VANILLA
1 tsp. BAKING POWDER	

In a small saucepan, heat butter and milk until butter is melted; set aside. In a mixing bowl, stir flour and baking powder together. In another bowl, combine eggs and sugar. Alternately add heated liquid and flour mixture to egg mixture, stirring well after each addition. Stir in vanilla. Pour batter into a greased tube pan and bake at 350° for 1 hour or until toothpick inserted into center comes out clean.

Bedford

Home to Poplar Park and the world's largest yellow poplar trees. One tree, listed in the National Registry of Champion Trees, is over 146 feet tall and more than 400-years-old!

Strawberry Pie

"My mother's dear friend, Edith Smith, gave her this recipe. We all love this pie!"

Innocent Wilson Moss—Bedford

1 cup SUGAR
1 box (3 oz.) WILD STRAWBERRY JELL-O®
4 Tbsp. CORNSTARCH
2 cups HOT WATER
2 (9-inch) baked PIE SHELLS
1 qt. fresh STRAWBERRIES, sliced
WHIPPED TOPPING

In a 3-quart saucepan, mix sugar, Jell-O and cornstarch. Add hot water. Heat on medium, stirring until mixture begins to thicken. Remove from heat and cool slightly. Pour into pie shells, add strawberries and refrigerate until set. Garnish with additional strawberries; top with whipped topping.

Virginia Food Festival Sampler

FEBRUARY—Chocolate Lover's Evening—Smithfield

MARCH—Highland Maple Festival—Monterey. **Whitetop Mountain Maple Festival**—Whitetop.

APRIL—Danville Wine Festival—The Crossing, Danville. **King William Ruritan Club Fish Fry**—Manquin. **Herbs Galore**—Maymont, Richmond. **Prince George County Heritage Fair**—Flowerdew Hundred. **Virginia Beef Expo**—Lexington. **Wakefield Ruritan Club Shad Planking**—Wakefield. **Graves Mountain Spring Fling**—Syria. **Central Virginia Historic Landmark**—Amherst.

MAY—Shenandoah Apple Blossom Festival—Winchester. **Seafood Festival**—Chincoteague. **Strawberry Festival**—Roanoke. **Heart of Virginia Festival**—Farmville. **Virginia Wine & Mushroom Festival**—Front Royal. **18th Century Spring Market Fair**—McLean. **Mt. Rogers Ramp Festival**—Whitetop. **Olden Days Festival**—Smithfield. **Nelson Farmers' Market Grand Opening**—Leesburg. **Chicken BBQ**—Emporia. **Seafood Fling at Fort Monroe**—Hampton. **Lebanese Food Festival**—Glen Allen. **Haymarket Spring Arts & Crafts Festival**—Haymarket. **Pungo Strawberry Festival**—Virginia Beach. **Strawberry Festival**—Heathsville. **Memorial Day Bull Roast**—Callao.

JUNE—Ashland Strawberry Faire—Ashland. **Virginia Pork Festival**—Emporia. **Seawall Festival**—Portsmouth. **Summer Fest on the Square**—Harrisonburg. **Virginia Chicken Festival**—Crewe. **Nelson County Summer Festival**—Oak Ridge Estate. **Harborfest**—Norfolk. **Ruritan Fish Fry**—Lawrenceville.

JULY—18th Century Summer Market Fair—McLean. **Pork, Peanut & Pine Festival**—Surry. **Virginia Cantaloupe Festival**—Turbeville. **Amelia Beef Festival**—Amelia. **Deborah Blueberry Fair**—Chincoteague.

AUGUST—Virginia Food Festival—Richmond. **Bayou Boogaloo & Cajun Food Fest**—Norfolk. **Virginia Peach Festival**—Stuart.

SEPTEMBER—Bay Seafood Festival—Kilmarnock. **Hampton Bay Days**—Hampton. **Rockbridge Food & Wine Festival**—Lexington. **Waverly Ruritan Beef Barbecue**—Waverly. **Boones Mill Apple Fest**—Boones Mill. **Haymarket Day**—Haymarket. **Virginia Peanut Festival**—Emporia. **Chilhowie Community Apple Fest**—Chilhowie. **Apple Harvest & Apple Butter Festivals**—Nelson County.

Virginia Food Festival Sampler (continued)

OCTOBER—**Great American Food Fest**—Chesapeake. **West Point Crab Carnival**—West Point. **Harvest Festival**—Kiptopeke. **Chincoteague Island Oyster Festival**—Chincoteague Island. **Virginia Garlic Festival**—Amherst. **Central Virginia Pork Festival**—Richmond. **Poquoson Seafood Festival**—Poquoson. **Sorghum Molasses Festival**—Clifford. **Whitetop Mountain Sorghum & Molasses Festival**—Whitetop. **Suffolk Peanut Festival**—Suffolk. **Madison Harvest Festival**—Madison. **King William Shrimp Feast**—Manquin. **Town Point Virginia Wine Festival**—Norfolk. **Harvest Festival**—Lynchburg. **Fairview Christian Church Apple Butter Festival**—Madison

NOVEMBER—**Urbanna Oyster Festival**—Urbanna. **Chili Night in November Chili Cook-Off**—Hampton. **Christmas at the Market**—Lynchburg.

DECEMBER—**Colonial Christmas Celebration Days**—Amherst

Product Resource Guide

Ann's Apple Butter
915 Etzler Road
Troutville, VA 24175
540-992-1881

Casey's Seafood, Inc.
807 Jefferson Avenue
Newport News, VA 23607
757-928-0257
www.caseyseafood.com

Delisheries, Ltd.
207 Mason Avenue
Cape Charles, VA 23310
800-524-8883

S. Wallace Edwards & Sons, Inc.
P.O. Box 25
Surry, VA 23883-0025
757-294-3121
www.virginiatraditions.com

Millcroft Farms Company
P.O. Box 138
Stanley, VA 22851
800-778-4072
www.applecandy.com

Rowena's, Inc.
758 West 22nd Street
Norfolk, VA 23517
800-627-8699
www.rowenas.com

Shenandoah Growers, Inc.
3453 Koehn Drive
Harrisonburg, VA 22802
540-896-6939
www.freshherbs.com

Virginia Carolina Peanut
    Promotions
P.O. Box 8
Nashville, NC 27856
252-459-9977
www.aboutpeanuts.com

Willaby's Fine Sauces,
P.O. Box 1122
453 Rappahannock Drive
White Stone, VA 22578
800-377-3378
www.willabys.com

Index

Index (continued)

Index *(continued)*

Index (continued)

Virginia Cook Book Contributors

Elizabeth Adams—Nana's Cottage Bed & Breakfast, Lynchburg   21

Ann's Apple Butter, Troutville 22-23,   69

Dr. Frances N. Ashburn—Lancaster County School System, Lancaster   15-16

Carol Austin, Sutherlin   32

Linda W. Ayers, Goodview   16, 55

William Barnhardt—Willaby's Fine Sauces, White Stone   8, 38

Shelby J. (Adkins) Barton, Haysi   27, 74

Meryl Bernstein, Richmond   14-15, 30

Min Bernstein, Richmond   34

Marilyn Burnette, Gloucester   53

Jane Bryan, Abingdon   51

Jim Casey—Casey's Seafood, Newport News 57-63

Lilly S. Chambers, Foster   50

Betty Lou Collius, Clinchco   76

Gloria Corcoran, Abingdon   85

Dale P. Dailey, Hopewell   72

Alma H. Davis, Clintwood   84

Margie Marie Edwards, Birchleaf   82

S. Wallace Edwards & Sons, Inc., Surry   10-12, 35, 37, 70-71

Tammy Belote Elvenia, Keller   47

Dora G. Evans, Lynchburg   80

Martha Fearnow, Mechanicsville   49

Betty Fitzgerald, Lyndhurst   39

Betty Weatherholtz Fitzgerald, Bedford 78

Bea Golden, Tappahannock   21

Tenecia Ann Hackney, Birchleaf   73

Mary C. Haden, Hopewell   42

Jacqueline M. Hadden, Lynchburg   45

Lion Bill Hadden, Lynchburg   77

Richard R. Hanson—Rebec Vineyards, Amherst   33, 40

Patricia Henderson, Prince George 28, 56

Ginger Howell, Goodwin   85

Ann Hart, Bedford 36

Fran Hart, Bedford 48, 55

Beverly Busch Hunter, Bedford   81

Dorothy T. Hunter, Bedford   42, 83

Nancy Law—Linden Vineyards, Linden 30

Rebecca Lindway—The Inn at Monticello, Charlottesville   10, 13, 18, 24

Ivea J. Logen, Elberon   76

Susan Longyear—Fairlea Farm Bed & Breakfast, Washington   9

Teresa Maddox, Amherst   56

Deborah Marshall—Delisheries Ltc., Cape Charles   84

Millcroft Farms Co., Stanley 12, 20, 31

Virginia Miller, Charlottesville   75

Innocent Wilson Moss, Bedford   87

Mary Moyer, Waynesboro   82

Debbie Greene Mullins, Clinchco 78, 80

Brenna Myers, Flowerdew Hundred Foundation, Hopewell   46

Pat Narron, Chester   52

Virginia Pork Producers, Richmond 44

Debra W. Pershing, Hopewell   19

Barbara B. Pillow, Phenix   54, 86

Madge Quadros, Newport News   23

Gina Reed—Mrs. Gina's Herbs & Things, Roanoke   31, 34

Martha Ann Richards, Newport News 29

Linda Barrett Roark, Abingdon   72

Rowena's, Inc., Norfolk   9, 33, 38, 70

Peggy Semancik, Abingdon   41

Bettie P. Shelton, Petersburg   13, 24

Shenandoah Growers, Inc., Harrisonburg 8, 17, 36, 71

Kyma Simmons, Goodview   79

Carol S. Slater, Sandston   86

Myrtle Soles, Seaford   37

Caroline S. Taylor, Charlottesville   79

Virginia L. Thompson, Abingdon   77

Marian Thorowgood, Conway   54

Joann M. Vicars—Bristol Virginia Police Dept., Bristol   74

Virginia-Carolina Peanut Promotion Assn., Nashville, NC 63-68

Virginia Marine Products Board, Newport News   46

Virginia State Beekeepers Assn., Glen Allen   32

Marie Holdren Wagner, Bedford   43

Deanie A. Whelan, Wicomico Church 87

Elinor S. Wilson—Bunker Hill Foods, Bedford 44

Mary Ann Wilson, Bristol   53

Harold Witt II, Roanoke   73

More books from Golden West Publishers

NORTH CAROLINA COOK BOOK

Filled with family favorites as well as recipes that showcase North Carolina's specialty foods. *Sausage Pinwheels, Shipwrecked Crab, Scuppernong Grape Butter, Carolina Blender Slaw, North Carolina Pork BBQ, Rock Fish Muddle, Hushpuppy Fritters, Hummingbird Cake, Peanut Butter Pie* . . . and more!

5 1/2 x 8 1/2 — 96 pages . . . $6.95

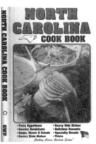

KENTUCKY COOK BOOK

Recipes from all across the great state of Kentucky! Try *The Derby Café's Mint Julep,* a *Benedictine Sandwich* or *Kentucky Derby Pie!* Sample many other favorites too, like *Kentucky Hot Brown, Poke Sallet* or *Cabin Grits Fritters.* Includes Kentucky facts and trivia.

5 1/2 x 8 1/2 — 96 Pages . . . $6.95

SEAFOOD LOVERS COOK BOOK

Recipes from coast to coast! Presenting lobster, crab, oysters, clams, salmon, swordfish, tuna, grouper, halibut and many more, featured in appetizers, soups, salads, side and main dishes. Includes seafood tips and trivia.

5 1/2 x 8 1/2 — 96 Pages . . . $6.95

BERRY LOVERS COOK BOOK

Berrylicious recipes for enjoying these natural wonders. From *Blueberry Muffins, Strawberry Cheesecake* and *Raspberry Sticky Rolls* to *Boysenberry Mint Frosty* or *Gooseberry Crunch,* you will find tasty recipes that will bring raves from your friends and family. Includes berry facts and trivia.

5 1/2 x 8 1/2 — 96 Pages . . . $6.95

APPLE LOVERS COOK BOOK

Celebrating America's favorite—the apple! 150 recipes for main and side dishes, appetizers, salads, breads, muffins, cakes, pies, desserts, beverages, and preserves, all kitchen-tested by Shirley Munson and Jo Nelson.

5 1/2 x 8 1/2 — 120 Pages . . . $6.95

ORDER BLANK

GOLDEN WEST PUBLISHERS

☼ 4113 N. Longview Ave. • Phoenix, AZ 85014

www.goldenwestpublishers.com • **1-800-658-5830** • FAX 602-279-6901

Qty	Title	Price	Amount
	Apple Lovers Cook Book	**6.95**	
	Bean Lovers Cook Book	**6.95**	
	Berry Lovers Cook Book	**6.95**	
	Chili-Lovers' Cook Book	**6.95**	
	Chip and Dip Lovers Cook Book	**6.95**	
	Corn Lovers Cook Book	**6.95**	
	Easy RV Recipes	**6.95**	
	Easy Recipes for Wild Game & Fish	**6.95**	
	Florida Cook Book	**6.95**	
	Joy of Muffins	**6.95**	
	Kentucky Cook Book	**6.95**	
	Mexican Desserts and Drinks	**6.95**	
	North Carolina Cook Book	**6.95**	
	Pennsylvania Cook Book	**6.95**	
	Pecan Lovers Cook Book	**6.95**	
	Pumpkin Lovers Cook Book	**6.95**	
	Salsa Lovers Cook Book	**6.95**	
	Seafood Lovers Cook Book	**6.95**	
	Veggie Lovers Cook Book	**6.95**	
	Virginia Cook Book	**6.95**	

Shipping & Handling Add: United States $4.00
Canada & Mexico $6.00—All others $13.00

☐ My Check or Money Order Enclosed

☐ MasterCard ☐ VISA

Total $ _____

(Payable in U.S. funds)

Acct. No. _____ Exp. Date _____

Signature _____

Name _____ Phone _____

Address _____

City/State/Zip _____

Call for a FREE catalog of all of our titles

3/04   **This order blank may be photocopied**   Virginia Ck Bk